INCREDIBLE STORIES FOR INQUISITIVE KIDS

Captivating Tales for Young Readers from History,
Science & the Crazy World We Live In

FRED FLYNN

INCREDIBLE STORIES FOR INQUISITIVE KIDS

Captivating Tales for Young Readers from History,
Science & the Crazy World We Live In

ISBN: 978-1-922590-60-2

CLAIM YOUR FREE AUDIOBOOK!

Get **instant access** to the
exclusive audiobook!

FLIP TO THE LAST PAGE TO CLAIM
YOUR BONUS...

TABLE OF CONTENTS

> Introduction 6

THE DAY THOMAS EDISON PIONEERED THE VERY FIRST
CAT VIDEO 8

AROUND THE WORLD IN MANY DAYS
AND IN MANY WAYS 10

> By Ship 10
> By Aircraft 12
> By Foot! 14
> By… Bubbly Hamster Ball? 16

A REMOTE ISLAND GETAWAY FOR ONE 19

A CHIP OFF THE CHOCOLATE BLOCK 28

THE GREAT KENTUCKY MEAT SHOWER 32

FLYING HIGH IN THE SKY 37

EXTREMELY ODD JOBS 42

> Knock, Knock! 42
> Hold Your Breath! 43
> Hold Your Nose! 43
> Be Quick! 44
> Super Storytelling! 45

THE UNSINKABLE WOMAN 46

BRAVING THE COLD 51

TWO MEDICAL MYSTERIES
FROM HISTORY 56

> The Dancing Plague 56
> The Laughter Epidemic 58

THE MOST CURIOUS CASE OF MARY MALLON 60

THE GREAT RACE OF MERCY 70

FIVE FASCINATING PETS 75

> Top Dog 75
> College-Bound Bear 76
> Remarkable Reindeer 77
> High Horse 78
> Steed of War 79

THE MECHANICAL CAMEL 81

THE MOST POPPABLE PRODUCT ON THE MARKET 86

THE LANGUAGE OF FREEDOM 90

WINNING THE SPACE RACE 96

THE GREAT MOLASSES FLOOD 101

ANGELS OF THE DEEP SEA 104

PLANTING FOR A PURPOSE 110

> Conclusion 114

INTRODUCTION

THE WORLD IS FULL OF STORIES, AND SOME SEEM too wild to be true, yet they are. In this book, you'll meet people and creatures who've done the impossible, survived the unimaginable, and invented the unthinkable. Welcome to a world where the extraordinary happens every day, and unbelievable tales come to life right before your eyes!

This is the magic of stories. Every day, new ones are being made, both fictional and real. But the ones you'll find here? Every one of them is true. These stories will inform you, entertain you, and make you think a little bit about the incredible world we live in. By the time you reach the last page, you might just see that reality can sometimes surprise us more than fiction ever could.

In these pages, you'll be transported to 1894 to watch the first-ever cat video. And who was the genius behind it? Well, you'll have to read on to find out. Next, you'll read about a brave dog who leads a daring rescue across the frozen wilderness of Alaska.

Then you'll meet Violet Jessup, the unsinkable woman who survived not one, but three shipwrecks, including the infamous Titanic. Discover how the beloved chocolate chip cookie came to be, or learn about the strange jobs that people have held throughout history.

From flying high in the skies with Queen Bess to braving the deep seas with Yvonne, each story has something new for you to learn about.

For your ease this book has been designed so you can read it any way you like. You can go cover to cover, or skip around and read the stories that catch your eye. Each one is short enough to read in a few minutes, and we've added bite-sized facts along the way to keep things fun and interesting.

You'll laugh, you'll gasp, and you'll probably say, "That can't be true!" But trust me—it is. So, turn to the next page.

LET'S EXPLORE THE
INCREDIBLE TOGETHER!

THE DAY THOMAS EDISON PIONEERED
THE VERY FIRST CAT VIDEO

CATS. THEY'RE FURRY, ADORABLE, AND HAVE TAKEN over the internet. For years, cat videos have been entertaining people all over the world. But have you ever wondered how it all started? Would you believe that the very first cat video was made way back in 1894? And that it was created by none other than the great inventor, Thomas Edison?

That's right, folks! The man who invented the lightbulb and the phonograph was also responsible for kickstarting the internet's favorite pastime. How incredible is that?

So, let's set the scene. It was the late 19th century, and Thomas Edison was a very busy man. His laboratory in Menlo Park, New Jersey, was always buzzing with new ideas and inventions. One of his most significant creations during this time was the Kinetoscope, an early motion picture device that allowed people to watch short films through a peephole viewer.

Now, Edison needed content to showcase the capabilities of his amazing new invention. So, he decided to film a variety of short scenes that would appeal to the general public. And what better subject than something that was both cute and amusing? Cats!

Enter "The Boxing Cats," the very first cat video in history. Edison's film featured two cats, dressed up in tiny boxing gloves and miniature boxing shorts, play-fighting in a miniature boxing ring.

A man, likely one of Edison's assistants, stood in the background, acting as a referee for the feline match.

Each round of the cat boxing match lasted only a few seconds, and the entire film was less than a minute long. But those brief moments of feline fun were enough to captivate the viewers of the time. People lined up to watch Edison's Kinetoscope and were delighted by the antics of the boxing cats.

And just like that, Thomas Edison had created the very first cat video, paving the way for the countless cat videos that would eventually take over the internet more than a century later.

Imagine if Edison knew that his short film would inspire millions of people to film their own cats doing funny, adorable, or downright bizarre things.

It's quite possible that he would have been amazed, but also quite proud, that his invention had brought so much joy to people worldwide.

So the next time you're watching a hilarious cat video, remember that it all started with a brilliant inventor and two boxing cats in 1894. Thank you, Thomas Edison, for giving us the gift of cat videos!

AROUND THE WORLD IN MANY DAYS AND IN MANY WAYS

Have you ever seen the movie Around the World in 80 Days? Perhaps you've read the book the movie's based on that was written by Jules Verne. If not, it's a great adventure story. Just know that it's fiction. But there are real people who have attempted to travel around the world throughout history and some who have even succeeded—multiple times! They're called circumnavigators and their stories are just as fascinating as any work of fiction. Let's discover some of the most interesting people who tried to go around the world and how they accomplished their circumnavigations of the globe.

BY SHIP

> THE FIRST FULL CIRCUMNAVIGATION HAPPENED between the years 1519 and 1522. It was a Spanish ship voyage that started in Seville Spain, went down and around South America, across the Pacific Ocean, past a bunch of islands, then across the Indian Ocean, around the southern tip of Africa, and back up to Spain. Phew, what a long trip!

Initially, the Portuguese explorer Ferdinand Magellan led the voyage, but he was killed in the Philippines and Juan Sebastián Elcano took over. That's why this voyage is called the Magellan-Elcano expedition.

> **THE ENGLISH PRIVATEER FRANCIS DRAKE COM**pleted another trip around the world in 1580. It had also taken him three years.

> **SIX YEARS AFTER THAT, THOMAS CAVENDISH,** another English explorer and privateer, shaved nine months off of Drake's time. On his second circumnavigation attempt, though, Cavendish died at sea.

> **THE 17TH CENTURY SAW MANY DIFFERENT TRIPS** around the globe, including by William Dampier, whom we'll meet briefly in our next story. Dampier didn't just travel the world once, or twice, but three times! He also was the first Englishman to explore parts of the continent that would later be known as Australia.

> FROM 1769 TO 1779, CAPTAIN JAMES COOK went on three long sailing expeditions. He mapped out many of the Pacific islands and other regions and was killed in Hawaii during his third voyage.

> THEN IN 1790, THE FIRST AMERICAN CIRCUM-navigation was completed by fur trader Robert Gray.

MANY OTHER SUCCESSFUL TRIPS BY SHIP OR SAIL-boat have occurred since then. But with the rise of aviation technology, a new form of transportation made the trip much quicker. And safer.

Well, kind of safer.

BY AiRCRAFT

> THE FIRST AIRBORNE CIRCUMNAVIGATION OF THE globe was in 1924 and took 175 days. Two different biplanes were flown by pilots in the United States Army Air Service. Obviously, this meant it wasn't a non-stop flight.

That wouldn't happen until 1949. The American Air Force plane *Lucky Lady II* made the trip in 94 hours and 1 minute. We're getting faster, folks. That's a big difference from three years aboard a ship.

> IN 1957, THOSE 94 MINUTES WERE CUT IN half when three Boeing B-52 Stratofortresses (jet bombers) completed a circumnavigation in just 45 hours and 19 minutes. The average speed of their flight was about 525 miles per hour!

> GERALDINE MOCK BECAME THE FIRST WOMAN TO complete a solo circumnavigation by plane in 1964. Sadly, Amelia Earhart had attempted this in 1937, but disappeared over the Pacific Ocean before she could make it.

> LOTS OF OTHER PILOTS HAVE SUCCESSFULLY circumnavigated the planet, and not just in planes.

> BACK IN 1929, THE AIRSHIP *GRAF ZEPPELIN*, guided by Hugo Eckener, made the trip in just 21 days. At the time, it was the fastest anyone had made it around the world, being before the advent of speedy planes.

> SEVENTY YEARS LATER, THE FIRST NON-STOP balloon circumnavigation took 19 days. It was completed by Bertrand Piccard and Brian Jones, whose time would soon be beaten. Piccard also was on the first solar-powered aircraft to circle the earth in 2016. But let's go back to the balloons for a minute.

> STEVE FOSSARD MADE THE TRIP IN A HOT AIR balloon in just 13 and a half days. Yet Fyodor Konyukhov broke his record in 2016 when he made it in 11 days.

> **A** DIFFERENT TYPE OF RECORD IS HELD BY Mack Rutherford, though. He became the youngest person to fly solo around the world in 2022. Mack was only 15 at the time, and his sister Zara Rutherford holds the record for the youngest woman pilot to complete a circumnavigation.

TODAY, YOU COULD PLAN TO FLY AROUND THE WORLD by getting tickets for connecting flights. Well, you could if you had a lot of money, that is. Yet people still like to sail around the world, or, as we'll see, walk or run.

BY FOOT!

OBVIOUSLY, YOU CAN'T WALK ALL THE WAY AROUND the world because of the oceans. So far, there are no bridges that connect every continent, so the trip is impossible. However, there are several people who have become pedestrian circumnavigators.

> **THE GUINNESS BOOK OF WORLD RECORDS STATES** that to qualify to be one of these extraordinary humans, you must travel on foot across four continents for at least 18,000 miles. For the rest of the voyage, you can take motorized transportation to get over large areas of water.

Still, 18,000 miles is no joke!

> **ATTEMPTS AT ON FOOT CIRCUMNAVIGATIONS** began in the late 1700s. But the first person to be successful at the journey was Konstantin Rengarten, who took over four years to get back to his starting point in 1898.

> **HOWEVER, DAVE KUNST WAS THE FIRST PERSON** whose trip was verified. He walked around the world between 1970 and 1974, though it's been reported that he rode a mule for some of the way.

> **THE NEXT DECADE SAW THE FIRST PARAPLEGIC** athlete, Rick Hansen, to make it around the world in a wheelchair. He traveled through 34 countries in a little over two years.

> **FYONA CAMPBELL BECAME THE FIRST WOMAN** to walk around the world, beginning her trip in 1985 and going in stages until she finished in 1995.

> **FROM 1997 TO 2003, ROBERT GARSIDE BECAME** the first person to run around the world. He ran over 30,000 miles, including on six of the continents.

> **THEN IN 2007, JASON LEWIS COMPLETED** his long journey of 12 years. He was the first person to go around the world solely by human power. When crossing water, he pedaled in a boat, rather than using a motor or sails to propel him along.

OTHERS HAVE CYCLED ACROSS THE GLOBE ON BIKES or hopped from train to steamboat to plane, but all with the same goal: to complete a circumnavigation. However, some people have been more successful than others.

BY... BUBBLY HAMSTER BALL?

OVER THE LAST TEN YEARS, ONE MAN HAS MADE many different attempts to travel through the Atlantic Ocean in a very unique way. That man is Reza Baluchi and he created some kind of watercraft that he calls a "hydro pod" in which he's tried to travel.

The hydro pod looked like a giant hamster ball and kind of worked like one. It was self-propelled, meaning Reza had to move it himself. That didn't seem to be a problem, since he was a professional runner and cyclist, having set several records and once cycled through 55 countries with a team promoting world peace.

In 2003, Reza ran from Los Angeles to New York City to bring awareness about the misperceptions Americans had about Middle Easterners after the terrorist attack in 2001. He also attended several charity events and ran to raise money.

However, he's most famous for his hydro pod, the first of which he built using his savings and launched in 2014. For this trip, Reza wanted to travel 3,000 miles from Pompano Beach, Florida to Bermuda, then to Puerto Rico, and back again.

The US Coast Guard thought that his plan was too dangerous, especially in the craft he wanted to take. They headed out to find him when he activated some distress beacons just 185 miles north of his starting location.

Apparently, Reza had set off the beacons by accident, though the Coast Guard found him to be looking pretty tired. They rescued him and towed the badly damaged hydro pod back to shore.

Two years later, Reza built a new one and tried to make another trip. The Coast Guard didn't give him permission and even threatened to put him in prison if he tried it. Reza ignored them and set off from Pompano Beach, this time planning to travel to several different islands in five months before returning.

Two days after he set out, the Coast Guard spotted him. Reluctantly, Reza agreed to be brought back to land.

But just a couple months later, he tried again, this time being towed out to international waters by a friend.

The Coast Guard found him floating alongside another boat. Once again, they brought him back and even had him evaluated by a hospital.

In 2021, Reza tried something new. He wanted to reach New York City from Florida, propelling his hydro pod up the eastern coast. He expected this trip would take him about three weeks. He didn't make it this time either.

Reza and his hamster ball bubble washed up in another Florida county. He claimed that he had to stop his journey because his GPS had been stolen.

Then in 2023, Reza decided to cross the Atlantic Ocean from the US to London, England. He set off in August in his hydro pod and the Coast Guard spotted him about 70 miles off the coast of Georgia.

When they examined his watercraft, the Coast Guard found it to be unsafe. They also warned Reza that Hurricane Franklin was coming. However, Reza pulled out a knife and threatened to kill himself. The following day, when they came upon him again, he held up some wires and said he was going to blow himself up, though he later admitted there was no bomb in his hydro pod.

Finally, the Coast Guard managed to convince Reza to come back to shore, where he was charged with obstruction of boarding and violating rules. The day after his sentence, he was released on the condition that he may not get on board another ocean vessel.

Time will only tell if he follows the rules.

A REMOTE
ISLAND GETAWAY FOR ONE

If only the man in our next story had
Baluchi's bubble, he could have spared himself
many years of misery….

ALEXANDER SELKIRK DIGS HIS HEELS IN THE SAND as he glares at his captain in the fall of 1704. For a few weeks, the crew of privateers had been recovering from illness and near starvation on an uninhabited island, where no one lived. But now, Captain Stradling wanted to get back on the seas.

"I want to sail again, too," Alexander says, "but our ship isn't going to make it back to Chile. We're 420 miles away!"

The other crew members murmur their agreement.

Captain Stradling glances at his ship, the *Cinque Ports*, where it rests in the gentle waves of the bay. Sure, maybe a few worms were eating through the mast and the deck had a few holes in it, but when you live a swashbuckling life, you just have to go with the flow sometimes.

You just need to learn to ride the ocean waves.

"It looks fine to me," the captain states. "Just listen to me for once, Selkirk, and get back on the boat."

"You cannot be serious," Alexander says. "Our ship is in great need of major repairs!"

Captain Stradling had just about enough of the troublesome Scotsman by now. Alexander had been nothing but a pain in his side since they'd left London. He might have been a good navigator, but the captain is so tired of arguing with him about the food, the crew, the condition of the ship—*everything*.

"We'll get it repaired when we get back to Chile," Captain Stradling promises as he stomps across the beach toward the ship. "All aboard!"

"Haven't you been listening to me?" Alexander shouts. "We won't make it back to Chile...or any land for that matter. There are too many leaks!"

Captain Stradling wants to stick his fingers in his ears so he doesn't have to listen to Alexander anymore. Instead, he turns around, ignoring the navigator, and beckoning to the crew.

"C'mon, sailors," Captain Stradling calls. "We've stocked the ship with turnips, crayfish, and goats for us to eat on the way. Pack up everything else and let's get going."

The crew looks between their captain and navigator, clearly confused about the decision they were being forced to make.

Alexander stands with his arms folded across his chest, and one foot atop the chest that held his few belongings. "If any of you think you'll stand half a chance against a squall or enemy ship on this deathtrap, then you're more foolish than a sack of spoiled potatoes."

Captain Stradling takes a deep breath, his face growing hot with anger. "Enough of your grumbling, Selkirk!" he yells. "Get back on the boat now!"

Alexander refuses to budge. "No, you can't make me. I'd rather stay here where we'd have a better chance of sur-viving," he says. With that, he turns his back to the captain and sits down on top of his chest.

At first, rage begins to bubble up within Captain Stradling. But then he starts to calm down. Perhaps with someone as aggravating as Alexander, you should take a different approach and let him do what he wants.

"Fine, Selkirk!" the captain says. "Stay here then, if you're so concerned. We're going to get back to attacking ships." Captain Stradling laughs at his own joke, not thinking for a minute that anyone would want to stay on a deserted island in the middle of the Pacific Ocean. Certainly not Alexander, who apparently wants a life of luxury and comfort.

Well, then, he shouldn't have signed up to become a pirate. Er, privateer, which is different, of course. While pirates were horrible criminals, the English king had given Stradling and his crew permission to capture and plunder foreign ships.

They are at least doing it legally.

When the crew see their captain striding toward the ship, most of them hurry after him. The few stragglers eventually do the same. None of them want to be left behind.

Apparently, Alexander does.

So be it, then. Captain Stradling isn't about to beg him further. Besides, what does he care if Alexander doesn't want to go back to Chile with them? They'd be better off if he didn't.

Alexander stubbornly remains with his back to the ship. He's sure that Captain Stradling will come around and agree to make at least some repairs before they head out. The crew would convince him if he didn't decide to do that himself. After all, that was the only smart thing to do.

But after a few minutes, no one comes over to Alexander. He stands up and turns around and sees that everyone is back on board the *Cinque Ports*. And they're pulling up the anchor.

"Uh," says Alexander. He watches as the sails are unfurled. Even with holes, they will catch some of the wind.

"Wait!" Alexander jogs across the sand toward the water, his legs tiring quickly. "You can't maroon me here!"

He hates to give in, especially to someone like Captain Stradling who thinks he knows everything. However, staying alone on a deserted island would be just as bad as sinking with his crew on the ship. Wouldn't it?

"I've changed my mind!" Alexander hollers. "Wait!"

The *Cinque Ports* doesn't wait. Alexander watches in horror as the crew readies the ship for departure. He wades through the waves to reach it, but Captain Stradling orders the ladder to be pulled up before he can get there. He gives Alexander one last smug expression before heading to the wheel.

The wind begins to propel the ship away from the island.

"You turn that ship around right now, or I'll..." But Alexander can't finish his sentence, because he knows it's hopeless. The only thing he can do is head back to shore.

Once back in the dry sand, Alexander watches the *Cinque Ports* get tinier and tinier as it sails away. Now, he's completely alone. And he regrets his stubbornness.

At least he has his chest of possessions. There aren't many of them—just a few clothes, a Bible and some other books, a cooking pot, knife, hatchet, and musket. But that's all he really needs, right?

No, he learns quickly. He needs other people.

After just a few days, the loneliness he feels makes him miserable. At first, he sticks to the shoreline. He catches spiny lobsters and keeps his eyes out for any passing ships that might rescue him.

Soon, his clothes are nothing but tatters because of the tropical climate.

Thankfully, though, he doesn't have to worry about starvation or dehydration. There are plenty of goats on the island, left there by past visitors, as well as sea lions and seals. In fact, the seals drive him away from the beach.

Taking refuge in the jungle, Alexander finds living there to be easier. He makes new clothes out of goatskins, remembering the skills his father, a tailor, taught him. What does he eat? Wild turnips and herbs that he manages to find, as well as any meat he can catch. But there is a big problem.

Rats.

At night, hordes of rats attack Alexander so he can't get any sleep. He builds two little huts as shelters, but the rats still get at him. This won't do, so Alexander sets out to tame some of the wild cats on the island. They not only keep the rats at bay for him, but become his companions.

Now, he's not so lonely. Though he still misses human civilization.

When he's not playing with his new pet cats, he reads his books and sings hymns. It's not a bad life until he runs out of gunpowder.

No longer able to shoot prey, he has to chase them through the jungle.

Once, Alexander chases a goat and doesn't see the edge of a cliff until he's tumbling over it. He falls, landing on the goat, which probably saved his life. After about a day, Alexander is able to get back up and tend to his injuries.

He begins to lose count of how many days he's spent on the island alone. But at some point, he sees a ship coming to the island!

Alexander is thrilled. He goes running out onto the beach, barefoot and in his goatskin clothes. Finally! Some other people!

Then, he comes to an abrupt stop.

The ship is flying Spanish flags. If they catch him, a British privateer, they'd see him as an enemy. It wouldn't be good for Alexander.

So, he's forced to run back into the jungle and hide.

Unfortunately, he doesn't make it before he's spotted.

The Spanish sailors rush into the jungle after him, shouting and calling to each other. Alexander quickly scampers up a tree and crouches down in the thick leaves.

He tries not to make a sound, all the while his head is screaming at him. He had come so close to being rescued, but of course it had to be a Spanish ship. Just his luck.

After a few minutes, the sailors give up their search for him. Two of them come over to the tree where Alexander is hiding and begin urinating right under him!

Alexander holds his breath, praying they don't look up.

Luckily, they don't and the ship leaves a short time later.

The next time a ship comes, Alexander is more cautious. It's a good thing, because this ship is also flying Spanish flags.

Finally, after being alone for four and a half years on the uninhabited island, another ship stops by. This one is British and full of privateers, including William Dampier, who had hired Alexander as a sailor many years before.

Overjoyed, Alexander meets up with the men when they come ashore. He can barely speak, not only because he's so happy, but because he's almost forgotten how. You see, he hadn't spoken to a single person in over fifty months.

When he can talk again, Alexander explains how he'd been left on the island. Dampier tells him that the *Cinque Ports* had fallen apart at sea. Captain Stradling and some of the crew survived the shipwreck, but had been picked up by Spanish sailors. They had been in prison for a while.

It turns out that Alexander had been right all along. Now, he helps Dampier and the other men to catch some goats and find some fruit so they can recover from scurvy. When everyone is healthy again, they board the ship—with Alexander—and sail away.

What happens to Alexander then?

Well, he decides to still be a privateer. After helping take a few treasure galleons, he amasses quite a fortune and heads back to England after eight years of being away. He settles down and gets married, but comes to miss his alone time back on the island.

By this point, many people had heard about his years as a castaway. Articles are written about him and Alexander enjoys a short stint of fame. Yet when the chance comes to join the Royal Navy, he takes it. He wants to get back out on the sea.

In 1721, though, he catches yellow fever and dies from the disease. He's buried at sea, but his story lives on.

Several authors have been inspired by Alexander Selkirk's experiences, as well as those of other castaways. The most famous is Daniel Defoe, who wrote a novel called *The Life and Surprising Adventures of Robinson Crusoe*. You may have heard of it or seen one of the many movie adaptations based on the book.

In any case, the story of Alexander doesn't just inspire fiction, but can be an example of how a person can survive some very harsh circumstances.

Near the end of his life, Alexander often remarked how happy he had been by himself on the island, even though he missed people greatly. Sometimes, alone time can be nice, but of course, no one wants to be stranded for nearly five years, miles away from any other human, and with only goats and wild cats for companions. That would be a very lonely life indeed.

A CHIP OFF
THE CHOCOLATE BLOCK

What would Selkirk have done for some chocolate
chip cookies while he was going hungry on
a remote island? Too bad they didn't really exist
until a couple centuries later!

THERE ARE MANY MYTHS ABOUT HOW CHOCOLATE
chip cookies came to be. One is that a woman named Ruth
Graves Wakefield made them by accident when she ran out of
baking chocolate, but this story isn't quite true.

So, what is true, then?

Well, Ruth Wakefield is a key player in making the cookies
famous, but did she actually invent them? Probably not.

Chocolate chip cookies were most likely a natural
progression of baked desserts. The fact is that there were
advertisements for chocolate chip cookies during the 1920s,
when Ruth was still in college. However, they weren't wide-
spread until Ruth began baking them for her patrons.

You see, in 1924, a young Ruth received her graduation cer-
tificate from the Framingham State Normal School Department
of Household Arts. That's a mouthful, isn't it? Hopefully the
name of your school isn't this long.

Anyway, Ruth became a dietician and lectured about
different foods until she got married. Then her life changed.

"Let's run an inn," her new husband Kenneth said.

"What a lovely idea," Ruth agreed.

They looked around New England for the perfect place and found it in no time. Between the city of Boston and Cape Cod was an old toll house. That was like a lodge where people stopped on their travels, paid a toll, or fee, and rested their horses.

The Wakefields took their savings and bought the building. They called it the Toll House Inn and opened it in 1930. Which could have been disastrous.

This was right at the start of the Great Depression, when many people were struggling to make a living. But the location of the Toll House Inn made it popular. Ruth's food, especially her desserts, made it even *more* popular.

People from all over came to stay at the inn and taste Ruth's cakes and cookies. Famous celebrities at the time, like Eleanor Roosevelt, Cole Porter, and Joe DiMaggio even visited there. You may not have heard of them, but it would be like having Michelle Obama, Taylor Swift, and LeBron James come to your house for dinner.

The travelers especially loved Ruth's cookies and she began to experiment with different kinds. She claimed she dreamed about the chocolate chip cookie while on a flight back from Egypt. The myth, however, says she chopped up a Nestle chocolate bar (or chipped off small chunks) and put it in the cookie batter when she realized she didn't have any baking chocolate.

Regardless, she began to serve her new cookie to customers.

"Delicious!" one of them said.

"Delightful!" said another.

"Downright delectable!" said a third. Delectable means "yum, yum, yum!"

Ruth had an instant success on her hands. Her new cookies were called Toll House Chocolate Crunch Cookies and the chocolate company Nestle was very interested in the recipe. Let's face it, who wasn't?

"We'd like to make a deal with you," said the owner of Nestle. "How about we supply you with a lifetime of chocolate if you allow us to print your recipe on our packages?"

"Deal," said Ruth.

It didn't take long for Nestle to realize just how popular these cookies were. Their sales of chocolate zoomed off the charts. So, they decided to make a whole new product: chocolate chips.

Now bakers didn't have to chop up the chocolate themselves. They could just throw a handful of chips right into the batter and pop it into the oven.

Even if she wasn't the first to come up with them, we have Ruth Wakefield to thank for inspiring Nestle and making chocolate chip cookies one of the best desserts in the world.

She came up with many more recipes, too, and wrote several cookbooks in her day. Yet she will always be remembered best for her delicious desserts.

THE GREAT KENTUCKY MEAT SHOWER

And now for another food-related story...
a much stranger one!

MRS. CROUCH HUMS AS SHE GOES ABOUT MAKING soap one March evening in 1876. The sky is crystal clear and the air is fresh. She's never been happier to live in Olympia Springs, Kentucky, where the climate is, for the most part, quite to her liking.

It is so nice that she even enjoys doing outdoor chores.

Swaying a little to her own humming, Mrs. Crouch uses her entire vocal range, going from deep thrums to high-pitched squeals.

But one of the hums gets caught in her throat as something falls from the sky and lands right at her feet.

"Goodness, me! Mrs. Crouch exclaims, clutching her pearls. For it had startled her quite a bit.

She looks up and sees something else hurtling toward her face. Mrs. Crouch sidesteps out of the way just in time. The object lands with a dull thud, right where she stood a second before.

Thud, thud, thud!

More of the same fall around the yard.

"What in tarnation?" she wonders. That's 1870s speak for "what the heck?"

Mrs. Crouch bends down to look at one of the objects on the ground. It is about the size of a large snowflake and looks like a chunk of beef.

"My Lord! A meat shower in the middle of March?" Truly, she would be surprised about it no matter the month. Things like this just didn't happen in Kentucky—or anywhere that she knew.

"Allen!" Mrs. Crouch shrieks to her husband. "Get out here! It's a sign from God!"

Mr. Crouch comes rushing out of the house, letting the screen door slam behind him. By the time he reaches his bewildered wife, he's pelted by three bits of flesh falling from the sky. But the strange phenomenon stops soon afterward.

Mr. Crouch scratches his head. "What's goin' out here?" he asks.

"I dunno. I was jis makin' some soap," Mrs. Crouch explains, "when it began raining meat!"

The next day, most of the neighbors had heard what happened at the Crouch residence. Mr. Harrison Gill decides to visit and sees first-hand that bits of meat were strewn all over the yard and stuck in the fence.

He examines them closely while Mr. and Mrs. Crouch wring their hands. They aren't sure whether it's a good sign or a bad omen from God.

"Well," Mr. Gill says, holding up one chunk of meat with his gloved fingers. "This is the largest one I can find."

It's about ten centimeters in diameter and most of the other pieces are half that size.

"Do you know why it fell from the sky?" Mr. Crouch asks.

Mr. Gill shakes his head. "I can't say for sure, but I should think it was quite fresh yesterday. After being left out all night, the meat now seems to be starting to rot."

Nevertheless, two other gentleman visitors decide to taste the meat to find out what kind it was. Better them than me.

"Reminds me of venison," says one.

"Really? I was thinking mutton," argues the other. "But you could be right."

The mystery of the meat shower remains just that for three months, when a man named Leopold Brandeis receives a few samples of the beef-like objects that had rained down. He pulls some out of the glycerin, a liquid used to preserve it, and looks at it closely.

After testing the meat, Mr. Brandeis decides it isn't meat at all.

"It's nostoc," he claims. "That is, it's a type of bacteria that swells up into what looks like a glob of jelly when it rains. Then, it falls down from the sky like hail."

"Oh, you mean witch's butter!" says one of the people he explains it to. "Or star slubber, isn't that what the folk say?"

"I guess," Mr. Brandeis says, raising his eyebrows. "Whatever you want to call it, it's not meat."

The problem is that Mr. Brandeis's theory doesn't make any sense, since it hadn't been raining the day that Mrs. Crouch witnessed the substance falling down in her yard.

Several other scientists are called upon to look at the samples. They conclude it is indeed some type of flesh. Three of the specimens appear to be muscular tissue, two are lung tissue, and two are cartilage.

Now the question is how and why did the flesh shower fall from the sky?

Enter Dr. L.D. Kastenbine. He takes a specimen and sets fire to it. Then, he sniffs the air. It's pretty stinky.

"Hmmm. Smells like rancid mutton," he says. "And the only explanation for what happened is that the chunks of meat came from the disgorgement of some vultures that were sailing over the spot. From their immense height, the particles were scattered by the wind over the ground."

In other words, the meat is *vulture vomit*.

Both the black vulture and turkey vulture can be found in Kentucky. Sometimes, they will vomit up their food to make themselves light enough to fly.

That's the best idea we've got to explain the Great Kentucky Meat Shower.

So, if you're ever in that state, be on the lookout for falling chunks of flesh that vultures might be throwing up. Try to dodge out of the way just as Mrs. Crouch did.

FLYING HIGH IN THE SKY

Meat may have rained down in Kentucky,
but half a century later, one young woman
dreamed of going up in the sky. She would face
extreme challenges in her attempts to get there.
Find out if she makes it or not.

WAY UP IN THE AIR IS WHERE BESSIE COLEMAN feels she belongs. The thrills and the sense of freedom she gets cannot be matched anywhere else, especially in the 1920s.

Especially for a Black woman like her.

Few others had the opportunity to become a pilot. In fact, Bessie is the first African American woman to do so, though she had to train in France because no pilot school would accept her in America.

Yet she found a way to make her dream come true.

And now she can go up in the sky and fly among the clouds, which, in her experience, is the only place free from prejudice.

While thousands of people watch down on land, Bessie does a barrel roll in her biplane, then dips down toward the ground. She imagines the audience gasping as she maneuvers the plane just in time to curve back up before hitting the earth.

Ever since she started performing flight shows, her tricks have gotten more daring. She guides the plane into a figure eight, then makes several loops.

INCREDIBLE STORIES FOR INQUISITIVE KIDS

Bessie is having so much fun that she doesn't want to land. Yet the air show is almost over.

After giving her fans a few more stunts, Bessie lands the plane perfectly and hops out of it. The crowd cheers and waves at her.

"Brave Bessie!" they chant. "Queen Bess!"

A couple men approach her and ask if she'll fly in other arenas.

"Only if they're desegregated," Bessie tells them. "I refuse to put on a show in a place where white people and Black people cannot come through the same gate or sit in the same seats."

This is one of the ways Bessie uses her fame to fight injustice. Her ultimate goal is to open a flight school in the United States so that African American women can learn to fly planes and experience the same sense of freedom she enjoys.

If she hadn't become a pilot, Bessie knows she would never have become so famous. Born in Texas in 1892, she had 12 siblings that had all worked in the fields picking cotton like her. She always wanted more for herself. So, she went out and got it.

Thankfully, she had help along the way.

Bessie will always be grateful for the people who loaned her money to go to France. In a weird way, she'd always be grateful to her brother, too, who once told her, "I know something that French women do that you'll never do...fly!"

Bessie decided right then and there to prove him wrong.

Now she's doing shows as an aviatrix, or female pilot. Not only that, but she's been called the world's greatest woman flier!

More and more people from all over the country want to see her aerial stunts, but Bessie sticks to her guns, refusing to perform anywhere that is segregated. She saves all the money she can so she can make her second dream of opening a flight school come true as well.

Sadly, she won't get the chance.

In April of 1926, Bessie is doing more stunts in the air, when she suddenly loses control of the biplane.

Her stomach drops. Three years ago, she'd gotten in an accident that left her with a broken leg and rib, and she doesn't want that to happen again. Those injuries prevented her from going up in the skies like she loved.

As her plane starts to plummet, Bessie desperately tries to ease it back up in the air.

It's not working.

Then, the plane begins to spin wildly.

Bessie Coleman, the greatest woman flier and first African American aviatrix, is thrown from her plane. She dies when she's only 34 years old.

It turns out that a loose wrench had gotten tangled up in the engine parts and caused the biplane to malfunction.

Fans of Bessie mourn her passing, but they are also inspired by her incredible bravery. She paved the way for girls and Black people everywhere to pursue careers, not only in aviation, but in other industries as well.

Seven decades later, in 1992, NASA astronaut Mae Jemison brings a picture of Bessie Coleman with her when she gets into a rocket and prepares for blast off. Mae becomes the first African American woman in space, and she carries on the legacy of the first African American woman in the skies. Both have become beloved idols.

WHAT FIRST
DO YOU WANT TO BE?

EXTREMELY ODD JOBS

Although being a female pilot isn't that odd anymore, when Bessie Coleman lived, she was quite a rarity. When it comes to things people do to make a living, there are, or in some cases were, even more unique jobs. While there have long been doctors, teachers, and firefighters, and will be well into the future, there are also occupations that are hard to believe anyone filled.

KNOCK, KNOCK!

How do you wake up in the morning? Do you have an alarm clock? Does your parent or guardian knock gently on your door or yell your name?

Believe it or not, there used to be people whose job it was to go around and wake others up. They were called knocker-ups or knocker-uppers because they used a stick or baton to knock on people's doors or windows.

Oftentimes, knocker-ups had to reach the windows on the second floor of a home, where the bedrooms were. So, they would need long, light-weight sticks, like those made out of bamboo. Some even used a pea-shooter to shoot dried peas at windows. Imagine having to wake up to that!

You see, people needed to get up and go to work in the days before alarm clocks existed or before you could really rely on them. So, they paid someone to do the job. That someone had to be an early riser, especially if they had lots of houses to wake up in the morning.

HOLD YOUR BREATH!

FOR MORE THAN TWO THOUSAND YEARS, THERE HAVE been women in Japan who are trained to hold their breaths for a long time while they dive down under the water. What are they doing? Collecting treasure from the ocean floor.

They are called ama pearl divers, and traditionally, they would gather food such as seaweed, abalone, and sea cucumbers. But they also brought up pearls and any other treasures they could find.

Sound like fun? Well, only if you're well-trained. From an early age, ama pearl divers practice swimming and breath-holding techniques that allow them to stay underwater for several minutes at a time. They learn how to slow down their heart rates and dive deep down in the water. Plus, they learn all about the environment of the ocean and seas and how to determine currents and tides.

The divers also must adapt to some frigid temperatures. Early on, they wore special suits called *isogi* which were made from cotton and helped protect bodies from the cold water, as well as jellyfish and sharks. This job was done long before diving equipment was invented. Yet even today, there are still ama pearl divers. The knowledge has been passed down from generation to generation, just like pearls themselves get passed down in other families.

HOLD YOUR NOSE!

DO YOU HAVE A DOG? DO YOU LIKE PICKING UP ITS poo after it goes to the bathroom? Few people do, but it's one of those things that has to be done. But what if you got paid to do it?

Seriously, that was a job at one time. The people employed to gather dog poo in Victorian England were called pure-finders. Apparently, dog poo was called pure back then, probably because it was pretty useful.

Tanneries, which made leather for things like book covers, used pure as a drying agent. And they paid quite a bit for it, which made the job of pure-finder not too bad of a gig. If you could stand the smell of dog poo, that is.

BE QUICK!

WHEN YOU GO BOWLING TODAY, A MACHINE SETS up the pins after they're knocked down, and also sends your ball back to you. But there weren't always machinest to do this job. Before 1953, people actually worked as pinsetters. Not just any people either, but children.

Pinsetters would get in position at the end of a bowling lane, working as fast as they could to set up the pins that players knocked down. They would also send balls back so they could be rolled down again.

Most pinsetters were pre-teen boys. In fact, they were often called pin boys. However, during World War II, some girls took up the job and they were called pinettes.

Being a pinsetter wasn't necessarily easy or safe. Sometimes, the workers would get hit with a ball or pin, even needing stitches for their wounds. One twelve-year-old had a finger get stuck between two balls. The injury was so bad, the finger had to be amputated, or cut off.

Eventually, the job of pinsetter no longer existed, because machines replaced the boys and girls who did the task. At least machines don't have to get stitches or amputations!

SUPER STORYTELLING!

AND NOW, FOR A SPECIALIZED JOB THAT NOT ONLY comes with a lot of responsibility but is also part of the position holder's identity. For many centuries, griots in West Africa have passed information through a blend of storytelling, singing, and announcement making.

It is the duty of a griot, pronounced GREE-oh, to keep the story about their village or tribe alive. They use oral tradition to pass down histories and preserve family trees. In this way, they are like walking, talking newspapers, relaying events like births, marriages, wars, deaths, and other events.

In another way, griots are like the bards or troubadours from the Middle Ages in Europe. Many of them play instruments while they dole out information or tell tales through song. In the past, griots would follow a king or emperor and act as their advisor, as well as entertainer.

How does one become a griot? Well, you typically have to inherit the job. Most of the time, griots only marry other griots and train their children to take over as storytellers after them.

DO MEMBERS OF YOUR FAMILY PASS DOWN ANY SKILLS OR JOBS?

WHAT HAVE YOU LEARNED FROM THEM?

THE UNSINKABLE WOMAN

Pinsetting could be a dangerous job, and so could pearl diving. How about being a stewardess on board a ship? Well, some people might not think it's that dangerous of a job, but the life of one young woman who worked as a stewardess was in danger several times.

VIOLET JESSUP STOOD ON THE DOCKS, STARING UP at the giant ship *Olympic*. It was way more impressive than the last ship she'd worked on as a stewardess, taking care of the passengers. She was lucky to have gotten this job with White Star Line.

Yet Violet didn't realize just how much luckier she would become.

The *RMS Olympic* was the first built of three new luxury liners. It had been built in Violet's parents' home country of Ireland. Though Violet had been born in Argentina, she had moved with her Irish family to England after the death of her father. By 1911, with her mother falling ill, she had joined the White Star Line and now boarded the *Olympic*.

It was a beautiful ship and even as a stewardess, Violet felt like she was living a life of luxury. She could only imagine what the big ship's two sister vessels would be like when they were done being built.

Not soon after the *Olympic* sailed out of Southampton, though, there was a loud noise and a violent jolt.

"Yikes! What was that?" Violet wondered. She rushed out onto the deck to see what was going on.

The *Olympic* had collided with another ship! And not a small ship either, but the *HMS Hawke*, a Royal Navy destroyer.

There appeared to be quite a bit of damage done to both ships. The *Olympic* had to abandon its trip and go back to Belfast for repairs.

Thankfully, it didn't sink.

But the *Olympic's* sister ships wouldn't be so fortunate.

Violet couldn't have known this, though, so she accepted a position on the second luxury liner. The name of this ship was the *RMS Titanic* and it headed out on its first voyage in April of 1912.

Sadly, this would also be the *Titanic's* last voyage.

It was nearly midnight when Violet was getting ready for bed. Suddenly, she heard a thunderous bang and a sharp screeching noise.

"Oh, no! Have we collided with another ship?" She hurriedly got dressed and went up to the deck, fearing it was going to be similar to what happened to the *Olympic*.

In fact, it was much worse. The *Titanic* had struck a massive iceberg and it was slowly starting to go down.

"Put on your life vests!" someone was shouting. "And head up to the top deck."

Violet did as she was told, watching as women hugged their husbands tightly before getting into lifeboats with their children. Her heart was racing with fear and she shivered from the cold.

Along with some of the other stewardesses, Violet was told by a ship's officer to get in one of the lifeboats to show people it was safe.

Again, she obeyed, and others piled in behind her.

Just as the lifeboat was being lowered into the water, the ship's officer thrust a baby in Violet's arms. She held tight to the infant, trying to keep it warm as the lifeboat was rowed away from the sinking luxury liner.

Nearly 1,500 people died with the sinking of the *Titanic*. Violet wasn't one of them, though she and the baby were freezing when a rescue ship came into view. It was the *RMS Carpathia* and it picked up her lifeboat three hours after she'd gotten on it.

She climbed up to the deck of the *Carpathia* carefully, still holding the baby. But as she stood around, looking to see if anyone needed help, a woman rushed by her and snatched the baby from her arms. Violet never saw it again.

The *Carpathia* took the survivors of the *Titanic* to New York. Violet only stayed there for a short time before returning to Southampton.

Incredibly, she decided not to change careers but still worked as a ship stewardess.

Two years later, the first World War broke out. The *Britannic*, which was the last of the three luxury liners, was used as a hospital ship to carry wounded troops,

Violet joined the Red Cross and went to work on the *Britannic*. During the ship's fourth trip in 1916, it ran into a mine planted by a German U-boat.

An explosion rocked the ship!

It began to flood, just like the *Titanic* had. Violet got into a lifeboat, feeling like she was going through a scary experience for the second time.

The *Britannic* was listing to one side, and its huge propellers were lifted out of the water. They spun dangerously.

The lifeboats began heading right for those propellers.

Violet wasn't about to get cut up by them. She jumped overboard into the sea but hit her head hard on something.

With hazy vision, Violet watched in horror as the lifeboat she was just on got chopped up by the propellers. Then the engines of the *Britannic* died and the propellers came to a stop.

Violet was pulled out of the sea as the third of the mighty ocean liners sank, just like its sister, the *Titanic*. With a mighty roar, the Britannic plunged down into the depths to rest at the bottom of the sea.

If you were Violet, would you stop working as a ship stewardess now?

Well, she didn't. For many more years, she worked aboard ships cruising around the ocean, until retiring at age 61.

She suffered from frequent headaches and one doctor she saw told her that she must have fractured her skull when she hit her head.

But that didn't stop Violet. Unlike the *Titanic* and the *Britannic*, she was truly unsinkable.

And she wasn't the only one.

Arthur Priest worked as a stoker who tended the fire that kept the steam engines running on ships. He was on board the *Olympic*, the *Titanic*, and the *Britannic* and even survived two other ship catastrophes besides.

When accidents happen, it's always horrible, but we usually try to learn from the past and put more safety measures in place. Sometimes, there's nothing us humans can do about nature, except try to be as brave and resilient as Violet Jessup.

BRAVING THE COLD

There are few survival stories as incredible as Violet's, but one man suffered through an impossibly cold night and shocked the world with his determination to stay alive.

MYLES OSBOURNE GLANCES OVER HIS SHOULDER to make sure the rest of his team is also making it up the mountain behind him. Indeed, his Sherpa guide and two fellow climbers are right on his tail.

It's not yet 9am on the 26th of May, 2006. Myles' team has been making good progress during this expedition up Mount Everest. They will soon be at the Second Step, a rocky out-crop on the northeast ridge of the tall mountain. They're over 28,000 feet high, which is hard for Myles to fathom though he's climbed the whole way.

Pulling himself up on the landmark known as Mushroom Rock, Myles is surprised to see a very unexpected sight.

A man is sitting to his left, cross-legged and changing his shirt. In freezing cold weather and high winds.

He's only a couple feet from a 10,000 foot drop and he hardly has any gear with him.

No sleeping bag. No sunglasses. No hat or gloves.

Most shocking of all is that he has no oxygen tank and regulator.

When you're at such high altitudes, the air is much thinner and there is less oxygen to breathe. It's essential that you bring enough oxygen with you when you are climbing a mountain as tall as Mount Everest.

Somehow, this man is still breathing. He turns to Myles and the other climbers coming up the ridge.

"I imagine you're surprised to see me here," he says.

Myles can only stare in disbelief for a few seconds. Here's a man who must have spent the night without oxygen or proper equipment and barely any clothes. How is he still alive?

Over 330 people have died trying to climb Mount Everest over the years. It is the highest mountain in the world and the climate near the top is extremely cold and windy. Even so, many mountaineers want to reach the top every year. It's usually the number one goal of climbers.

When people go on expeditions up Mount Everest, they typically hire a guide from among the Sherpa people, just like Myles and his team did. The Sherpas have lived in the Himalaya mountain range for many generations and know how to navigate the treacherous terrain and survive the harsh weather.

Myles and his fellow climbers learn that the man's name is Lincoln Hall. He had been on his way down from the peak the night before with his own team. Yet he collapsed and he's not sure what happened to them.

Though Lincoln survived the night, he's not in the best shape. Not only is he severely dehydrated without having any water, but he's not making any sense when talking to the other men. They realize he must be suffering from cerebral edema, or brain swelling. He appears to be hallucinating, or seeing things that aren't actually there.

Not only that, but Lincoln has a bad case of frostbite.

Myles and his team decide to abandon their summit up to the top of the mountain so they can help Lincoln. They give him oxygen, food, and water out of their own supplies, even though they might not have enough left for their own trip back down.

Over the radio, they are able to contact Lincoln's climbing team from the day before. They're just as shocked to hear he's alive as Myles was when finding the man.

It turns out that Lincoln collapsed as his team was descending from the summit of the mountain. For several hours, his team members, along with their Sherpa guide, tried to revive him. Other Sherpas were called to help with the rescue but no matter what they tried, Lincoln was unresponsive.

Once night began to fall, they had to leave Lincoln behind. They were running out of oxygen and it would be very dangerous climbing down at that time of day. By this point, the rescuers pronounced Lincoln dead. As soon as they returned back to camp, the expedition leader called his family to tell them the sad news.

But Lincoln had miraculously survived. Myles and his companions stay with him until a rescue team of twelve Sherpas reaches them from a base camp on the mountain.

They bring Lincoln down the mountain and back to the camp, where a Russian doctor examines him.

Luckily, Lincoln only has to lose one toe and his fingertips to frostbite. He makes a full recovery otherwise.

While his fingers are still bandaged up, he begins writing a book about his harrowing experience, which he titles *Dead Lucky: Life After Death on Mount Everest*. It's from this that we can learn just how he managed to survive.

Lincoln believed in Tibetan Buddhism. He was used to meditating and when extremely cold, he was able to slow down his heart rate and conserve energy. He was also well versed in the eight stages of death that are associated with Tibetan Buddhism and he thinks he went through two of the stages during the night he spent on the mountain alone.

The story of his survival has become both a warning and an inspiration to many other mountain climbers. Documentaries were made about him and in 2010, Lincoln Hall was given the Australian Geographic Society's Lifetime of Adventure award.

Few people have had to face such extreme elements before. Lincoln was all alone in one of the harshest environments on earth, yet he was resilient enough to come through his experience alive.

Let's hope that other mountain climbers don't have to go through such a terrible ordeal to reach their ultimate goal of climbing the tallest mountain.

WHAT iS YOUR TOP GOAL TO REACH?

TWO MEDICAL MYSTERIES FROM HISTORY

With the help of medical professionals, Lincoln Hall was able to recover from a night in the extreme cold. Yet even though we've learned a lot about medicine and the human body over the millennia, there are still some unexplained diseases. Here are two strange occurrences that people suffered from that have confused doctors and other experts for years. But there may be something of an answer to them...

THE DANCING PLAGUE

IN THE CITY OF STRASBOURG IN THE YEAR **1518,** a woman named Frau Troffea was struck by a sudden urge to start dancing. No one knew why, but when she stepped into the square, she began shaking her body and dancing uncontrollably.

There was no music, at least that anyone else could hear, and there was no stopping her. Truly, Frau Troffea couldn't stop, not even when she grew tired and achy. She just danced and danced until she actually collapsed from exhaustion. After resting, she would get back on her feet and begin dancing again.

This went on for several days, with other people joining her in this compulsive dancing. It seems that the affliction was contagious.

Soon, hundreds of people were dancing through the streets of Strasbourg, not even stopping when they injured themselves. Many of them had bloody feet and pulled muscles, but they kept on dancing.

The city didn't know what to do. They thought it might help if they provided a place for the dancers and had people playing instruments to accompany them. So, they opened guild halls, but this just seemed to make it worse.

Over two months, the dancing plague affected 400 people. Sadly, many of them died.

But then the dancing frenzy stopped, just as mysteriously as it started.

Strasbourg wasn't the only place where this happened either. There are multiple reports of dancing outbreaks that took place sometime between the 10th and the 16th centuries.

But what caused this strange compulsion? Back then, some religious people thought the dancers might be possessed by demons. Later, there was a theory that they had eaten rye bread which contained a fungal disease. One of the effects of this disease was to break out in convulsions.

The theory which is most accepted, though, is that the dancing plague was a form of psychogenic illness or mass hysteria. During extremely stressful times and events, people may lose bodily control and be overcome by certain impulses. And there was a lot to be stressed about during the Middle Ages, including poverty, war, and smallpox.

Could this explanation also work for another odd outbreak that occurred around 440 years later?

THE LAUGHTER EPIDEMIC

WE ALL LOVE TO LAUGH, BUT IT DOESN'T ALWAYS mean we're happy. Sometimes, we feel the urge to laugh when we're sad or angry or scared. Sometimes, we can't stop laughing, no matter how hard we try.

An epidemic of laughter broke out in Tanganyika in 1962. This is in East Africa and is now called Tanzania. At a girls' school there, some of the students began to laugh and just like the dancing in Strasbourg, they couldn't stop. It was uncontrollable.

The laughter spread from the school out into the village and then to other nearby villages. At least 1,000 people were affected and the laughter epidemic lasted for several months.

People would have a laughing or crying fit that could last for a few hours or many days. Some of them took off running, unable to control their movements. Schools were even closed down for a while in the hopes that the epidemic would end.

Again, it was thought that this might be a type of psychological behavior happening to a group of people under stress. Tanganyika is a famous example, but similar outbreaks to this have also occurred in other places like Afghanistan, Kosovo, and South Africa, as well as at a school in England.

While laughter can relieve stress sometimes, clearly it can also be a response when we feel anxious. When it becomes overwhelming, that's when it becomes dangerous.

Hopefully, in the future, we don't have to live with so much stress that we can't stop laughing or dancing. It's much better to do both of those to have fun.

THE MOST CURIOUS CASE OF
MARY MALLON

While the Dancing Plague and Laughter Epidemic don't seem as bad as some other horrible diseases in history, they were quite dangerous to human health. So was typhoid fever, which was pretty common at one time, when living conditions and advancements in science were far below what they are now. In fact, there was a mystery revolving around typhoid that ended up becoming a medical breakthrough.

A SMILE BREAKS OUT ON MARY MALLON'S FACE AS she glances up at the large summer house on Oyster Bay, Long Island. It's just lovely. A perfect place to work in 1906. And with her long record of cooking for upper class families in New York City, she shouldn't have a problem getting the job. No problem at all, right?

Well, there's that one thing...

There's the fact that some of the family members she cooked for happened to fall ill with typhoid fever.

But that wasn't her fault! It had nothing to do with her, especially since she had never gotten sick herself. Besides, she hadn't immigrated all the way from Ireland when she was a teenager just to live in poverty when she is perfectly capable of making a living as a cook.

Mary tells the butterflies in her stomach to calm down, straightens her spine, then heads into the house. She is immediately taken to the wealthy banker whom she hopes will be her new employer.

"Well, Mary," says Charles Warren a little later, "you seem to be just the type of cook my family is looking for. I'm impressed by your past jobs."

Mary's confidence soars. She had no reason to be nervous. She is a good cook after all, and has proven her skills time and again to many important people.

"Thank you, sir," she says.

"That's it, then." Mr. Warren gets to his feet and holds out his hand. "You're hired, Mary. I look forward to your meals."

Mary stands up from her seat and stretches out her arm, hoping that her palm doesn't feel too cold and clammy. They shake on it.

She had been anxious before, but is so glad that she'd be cooking for the Warrens. They promised a fair pay and if it worked out for the summer, perhaps she could go back with them to the city after their vacation was over.

"It'll be a pleasure to serve you, sir," Mary says. "A pleasure indeed."

And a pleasure it was...at least for the first week or so.

After each meal, the Warrens praise Mary's cooking as delicious, exactly as she'd claimed. They wonder how the other families could have possibly let her leave.

"Mary, you've done it again," says Mr. Warren one evening as Mary brings dessert to the table. "You're an absolute natural in the kitchen."

"Thank you for saying so, sir," Mary says. She beams at him and his family, though there are a couple missing members. She'd been told they weren't feeling well and that was concerning.

"It's such a shame that the whole family can't enjoy this meal," Mr. Warren laments. He takes a big bite of his dessert.

"I know," says Mrs. Warren. "Fancy coming down with a case of typhoid in Oyster Bay of all places!"

Oh, no, thinks Mary. No, no, no. It can't be happening again. Not so soon after she was hired!

Later that night, the other servants bustle around the kitchen making tea and wetting cloths to take to the sick family members. Six of them have now fallen ill. Six!

It didn't make sense. Typhoid fever usually affected poor people who ate or drank contaminated food and water. Cases were rare amongst the elite.

Unfortunately, this was an all too common event for Mary. While the other servants begin to panic, she slips quietly back to her room to pack her few things. She has to get out of there before she's blamed for the typhoid. Even though she knows it isn't her fault...

A few months later, Mary finds herself in a new kitchen in a new house. She hums to herself as she peeks in the oven to see how her meat is coming along. It looks nice.

"Excuse me, Ms. Mallon?"

Mary whirls around to find that a man has entered the room. "Yes?" she asks cautiously.

"My name is George Soper," the man says. "I'm a civil engineer who has been investigating the outbreak of typhoid fever in Oyster Bay."

A cold chill runs through Mary. "Oh," is all she says. But she holds out a hand for Soper to shake. He ignores it, which Mary thinks is rude. She gives him a steely glare.

Soper takes out a small notebook and pencil. "You used to work for the Warrens, correct?' he asks.

"Yes," Mary says.

"And for several other families, including the Kesslers and Gisleys."

"Yes."

"People in each of these households contracted typhoid fever."

Mary stands taller. "Probably from the water," she says.

"The water has been tested," Soper tells her. "We have reason to believe you might be the one spreading the disease and we would like to test your blood, urine, and uh, feces."

Mary's fair skin gets red with anger. "No," she says.

"Please, Ms. Mallon, we—"

Mary snatches up a carving fork from the counter. "I said no. You get out of here right now," she threatens.

Soper puts his hand up as Mary points the sharp fork at him. "Okay, okay," he says. "No need for that." He flees the kitchen while Mary tries to calm herself down.

She soon realizes it isn't that easy to get rid of George Soper. He comes back with a doctor to get her to agree to the tests. Mary refuses again.

"Typhoid is everywhere," she says. "The food and water can easily become contaminated. I'm not sick at all, so I obviously don't have it."

Is it so obvious, though? Soper proves that of the eight families Mary worked for, seven of them had people who fell ill. One young girl even died after contracting the illness. And he's sure Mary has something to do with it.

In March of 1907, the New York City Health Department determines that Mary is a public health threat. The authorities come to arrest her. At least, they try.

"Let go of me!" Mary yells as two policemen grab her arms. "I haven't done anything wrong!" She thrashes about, trying to get free.

"We need to take you in for testing," a doctor explains.

"There's no need! I'm not sick!" wails Mary. She's strong and struggles against the officers. It takes five of them to restrain her.

After some time, they finally get her in the back of an ambulance. But Mary isn't done fighting.

As soon as the officers let go of her, she lunges for the door to escape.

"Mary, please stop resisting," the doctor says.

Mary doesn't stop.

"This is like being in a cage with an angry lion," the doctor remarks. It gets so bad that she is forced to sit on Mary's lap until they get to Willard Parker Hospital.

Once there, doctors take stool and urine samples from Mary. When the results come back, there are indeed traces of the bacteria known to cause typhoid fever.

Today, we know how disease spreads between people. Teeny, tiny, microorganisms that can't be seen by the human eye pass from infected individuals to others. Good hygiene practices such as washing your hands often can help stop the spread of disease.

Back in 1907, people didn't fully understand germs. And they also didn't fully understand how Mary had typhoid bacteria but never showed symptoms of the sickness.

It turns out that Mary rarely washed her hands, even when she was cooking. Most people didn't back then. The bacteria in her body would contaminate the food she served to her employers and that's why so many of them fell ill.

"We're sorry, Mary," say the doctors, "but we can't risk you making people sick, so we will have to quarantine you."

"But I don't have typhoid fever," Mary insists.

No one listens to her.

She's sent to Riverside Hospital on North Brother Island, where more doctors examine her. They make her give samples several times a week. Since the bacteria is in her gallbladder, an organ that aids in digestion, the doctors wonder if they should remove it from her body. Mary refuses to have the surgery, which was very dangerous back then.

Besides, Mary didn't believe herself to be a carrier of the disease. She's miserable and feels like she's being treated like a prisoner. It gets even worse when the media finds out about her.

George Soper had published his findings and the newspapers began to report on Mary's condition. They even give her a nickname, "Typhoid Mary," and say that she's a dangerous woman.

This makes Mary feel like an outcast.

Soper visits her at one point and he's the last person Mary wishes to see.

"I'd like to write a book about you," he says. "I'll even give you some of the royalties."

Mary is upset about her reputation and she doesn't want it to get even more out of control. She rejects Soper's proposal and locks herself in the bathroom until he leaves.

Three years after she was quarantined on the island, Mary is finally offered a deal that could secure her freedom.

The state's health commissioner, Eugene H. Porter, lays out his terms. "Ms. Mallon, if, and only if, you are prepared to stop working as a cook, and you agree to take every possible precaution to prevent the transmission of your disease, then

I will discharge you from this hospital. You will be free to live your life as you please."

Mary scowls. She is certain she doesn't have typhoid and even tried to sue the New York Health Department, but her case had been dismissed. However, she wants out of quarantine. So, she agrees to the terms.

Instead of cooking, Mary becomes a laundry worker for a while. But she isn't paid as well as she used to be. So, she changes her last name and finds work as a cook in restaurants and hotels.

In 1915, there's an outbreak of typhoid fever at the Sloane Hospital for Women in New York City. At least 25 women fall ill, and two of them die.

George Soper is called in to investigate. Sure enough, he recognizes Mary Mallon from her handwriting.

She is arrested once again and taken to North Brother Island again. This time, she's given a private cottage to live in, where she spends the rest of her life. She continues to feel that she has been treated unfairly. And she continues to deny that she doesn't have typhoid fever, right up until her death in 1938.

Mary was identified as a carrier, meaning that she carried the bacteria but never showed symptoms of the disease. While many others were also found to be the same, some carrying even deadlier bacteria than typhoid, only Mary was treated this harshly.

Is it because she was a woman, an Irish immigrant and not a member of the upper class? We may never know. But we can surely understand how isolated she felt.

We can also understand how scary it is to have a disease spread without knowing why. To save our own health and the health of others, it's important to follow doctor's orders and keep our hands as clean as possible.

THE GREAT
RACE OF MERCY

*Instead of making people sick, Togo did his very best
to help those who had fallen ill. And his very best—
especially for a dog—was absolutely astounding.*

IT BEGAN TO SNOW AS LEONHARD SEPPALA PREPARED
his sled dogs to race across Alaska in 1925. Nicknamed Sepp, he
raised dogs to pull sleds and was one of the strongest mushers,
or dog sled racers in the region. Perhaps in the whole world.

But this was no usual race for a trophy or award. It was to
save the lives of many sick people.

No, they hadn't contracted typhoid fever. There was actually an outbreak of diphtheria, which is as dangerous as the
word looks. Diphtheria is highly contagious and can cause people to have trouble breathing and swallowing. If the infection
is left untreated, it can even cause death.

But don't worry. Today, we get vaccines for diphtheria when
we are young. Back in the 1920s, though, it was quite prevalent.
Children were especially vulnerable to the disease. That's why
Sepp was one of many mushers asked to deliver a serum that
could treat diphtheria.

And he would give it everything he had to get it to the sick
people as fast as possible.

"Sepp, that blizzard's coming in quick," one of his fellow mushers said, looking up at the falling snow.

"I know. The planes can't fly in weather like this. It's up to us."

"So, which of your dogs do you think should take the lead?"

There was only one Sepp had in mind. Togo, a smart, tough Siberian husky. At that time, Togo was 12 years old and one of the most intelligent and most determined dogs Sepp had ever raised in his kennel.

When Togo was just a puppy, though, Sepp thought he was too small and scrawny to be a good sled dog. Togo had many health problems and he was sent to a neighbor as a pet.

But that wasn't where Togo wanted to be.

He threw himself out a glass window. and ran several miles back to Sepp's kennel. So, Sepp decided to raise him, even though he didn't think Togo would be any good at racing.

Boy, was he wrong.

Togo the pup seemed fascinated by the much older and bigger sled dogs that Sepp trained. He would get loose from his kennel and go running alongside them.

Finally, Sepp decided to put a harness on Togo when was only eight months old. Then, he hooked the dog up to a sled team.

That first day, Togo ran 75 miles! Sepp was so impressed that he began to train him as a lead dog. It was a smart decision because he won all sorts of races with Togo. The Siberian husky became popular in Alaska for his amazing strength and endurance.

In 1925, you would think the 12-year-old Togo was past his best years, because that was pretty old for a dog of his breed. However, Sepp knew better.

None of his dogs would be able to lead a team as good as Togo. He hitched the Siberian Husky up, made sure everything was ready, and headed out.

The climate was freezing at -30 degrees Fahrenheit and the gale force winds made it feel much colder.

"We can do this," Sepp said to himself, hoping he was right.

Twenty teams of mushers were ready to help. The serum had been brought as far west as it could by train. But there were still 674 miles to Nome, where the people were sick. A dog sled relay was arranged to cover the distance.

When it was Sepp's turn, he encouraged his team, led by Togo, to run their hearts out. His dogs pulled his sled across the frozen land, against the winds. None of the huskies were very big. Togo was only 48 pounds. But they were mighty.

Sepp could hardly see because of the snow whipping his face. He knew he could rely on Togo's instincts, though.

Once, when they were trying to cross the Norton Sound, Sepp and his team got stuck on an ice floe. They floated in the water on a big chunk of ice and couldn't get across.

Sepp tied a line to Togo and tossed the dog over on the other bank. Togo understood exactly what to do. He began to pull the ice that held his team across the water.

But the line snapped!

Sepp began to panic. Luckily, his brave lead dog didn't.

Togo jumped in the water, grabbed the line with his teeth and rolled around so that it circled his body. Just like a harness. Then, he pulled his team to safety.

Togo was truly an incredible dog.

He proved it again during The Great Race of Mercy, which is what the media called the serum race. While most other teams made it about 31 miles apiece before stopping, Togo and Sepp

ran 260 miles over three days. That's more than the distance of 4,500 football fields!

The last 50 miles of the race was run by a team with Balto as the lead dog. You may have heard of Balto, who was also one of the dogs that Sepp bred and raised in his kennel. Balto has been praised for his part in the event. And while all of the dogs did an amazing job, Togo was the real hero of that trip.

The serum was delivered to the people who needed it. Since no trains or planes could get it there, the dogs stepped up, or stepped forward, rather, to get the job done.

Togo went with Sepp to tour the United States and ran a few more races in his day. Eventually, he retired and passed away in 1929.

It took several years for his contributions to The Great Race of Mercy to be recognized by the public. He finally got a statue made, just like Balto, and a movie made about him. The movie starred a dog named Diesel, who is actually one of Togo's descendants!

Sepp was one of many who knew what a special animal Togo was. He was always grateful that he had such a remarkable companion.

"I never had a better dog than Togo," he said. "His stamina, loyalty and intelligence could not be improved upon. Togo was the best dog that ever traveled the Alaskan trail."

FIVE FASCINATING PETS

As Togo has shown us, not all famous historical figures are human. There are some animals who have incredible stories, too. If you have any pets, I'm sure you love them dearly, but you probably can't imagine treating them like the ancient Roman emperor Caligula treated his horse, or bringing them to school, like Lord Byron brings his unusual pet!

TOP DOG

ONE OF THE TEENIEST, TINIEST TOWNS IN AMERica has become famous for its elections. Why? Because the winning mayoral candidates are always canines!

Here's the tale, or should we say, *tail*?

Back in 1998, Rabbit Hash, Kentucky decided to elect their first mayor. They held a contest in which people began paying a dollar per vote. Then someone thought a black Lab named Herb would make a good mayor, so they entered him into the race. Herb's campaign slogan was "The Perfect Politician—He Doesn't Talk!"

Well, Herb was cool and all, but the most popular dog in Rabbit Hash, *paws down*, was Goofy Borneman. A mutt who ran all over town, Goofy got hit by cars more than once and fathered about two hundred pups!

When Goofy entered the race for mayor, no one else stood a chance. That goes for all the humans, Herb the other dog, and even a potbellied pig.

With his win, Goofy became a fuzzy, four-legged celebrity. He was featured on the radio and television and even starred in a documentary. Though he passed away in 2001 at age 16, Goofy's legacy lived on.

Every mayor of Rabbit Hash since their first has also been a beloved dog. Other animal candidates like a rooster and a donkey have run for office, but every four years, the town makes sure that the position goes to the right dog for the job.

COLLEGE-BOUND BEAR

LORD BYRON, THE BRITISH POET, ALSO LOVED his pet dog. He was dismayed to find that when we entered Trinity College at Cambridge University in 1805, he wasn't allowed to bring his dog with him.

So, you know what he brought instead? A bear!

You can imagine that the school wasn't too happy about this. But Lord Byron, a 6th Baron (more like Bearon, right?), said that the rules didn't ban bears at the college. Cambridge couldn't argue with him. So, he was allowed to keep the bear.

There are reports that Lord Byron dressed up his unique pet in human clothes and walked him around campus like a dog. He also tried to enroll the bear as a student, but Trinity college didn't agree with him this time.

Besides his bear, Lord Byron kept many birds as pets, including peacocks, geese, a falcon, an eagle, and an Egyptian crane. He also had monkeys, as well as a fox and a badger. And of course, as most people did in the early 19th century, Lord Byron had horses. Yet his bear was the only pet to become almost as famous as him.

REMARKABLE REINDEER

DURING WORLD WAR II, THE BRITISH SUBMARINE *HMS Trident* was given a strange gift by the Russians. A reindeer! Can you believe it?

Just why they were given a reindeer has been debated.

One story says that Captain Sladen had dinner with the Russian admiral and remarked that his wife had a hard time pushing her pram, or stroller, through the snow. Well, the perfect solution to that would be to have a reindeer pull it.

But another story claims that the crew of *HMS Trident* were given a reindeer as a reward for fighting the Germans in the Arctic Circle.

Either way, Pollyanna the Reindeer found herself being lowered through one of the torpedo tubes into the submarine.

Now, most submarines are built to house people, not reindeer. Where should the crew put Pollyanna?

It was decided that she should stay in a storage area. However, that wouldn't do for Pollyanna. She liked the captain's cabin way better, so that's where she was allowed to stay. She even slept under the captain's bed!

The other problem was what to feed her. The Russians had sent a barrel full of moss with Pollyanna, but she ate that up pretty quickly. So, she was given leftovers from the mess hall, or cafeteria, on the submarine. She even tasted some navigation charts, though they weren't very nutritious for reindeer.

Pollyanna especially loved the condensed milk. For six weeks in the sub, she was given lots of milk and scraps and she put on some pounds. So many pounds that she was too big to back through the torpedo tube.

How to get her out of the submarine?

The only option was the main hatch. It took several members of the crew to hoist her out, and Pollyanna was finally back on land.

She was sent to the zoo, where she happily spent the rest of her years. However, Pollyanna never forgot her time on the submarine during the war. Every time she heard sirens, she would lower her head.

HiGH HORSE

So, IF THERE'S AN EMPTY SEAT IN THE SENATE, or ruling class, in ancient Rome, who should fill it? A horse, of course!

At least, that's what Rome's third emperor thought. Gaius Caesar Germanicus is much better known as Caligula, which was a nickname given to him that means "Little Boot." Caligula only ruled for four years, from 37 to 41 CE, but he was such an oddball, that he became one of history's favorite subjects. And so did his pet.

Caligula may not have liked many people, but he loved his white stallion Incitatus. Loved him so much, in fact, that he had a stable built out of marble for him. And an ivory manger which held Incitatus' food—only when he ate outside.

Sometimes, Caligula invited his favorite racehorse to eat dinner with him. The emperor fed Incitatus oats flecked with gold and had a collar of jewels made for him. He also commissioned purple blankets for Incitatus and ordered a group of enslaved servants to take care of the horse.

The evening before a race, if you lived anywhere close to Incitatus' stables, you had to be silent so you didn't disturb the animal. By the way, Incitatus means "swift" or "fast-moving," in Latin. A good name for a racehorse.

But what about being appointed to the Roman Senate? As far as we can tell, that didn't actually happen, though it was rumored to be true.

Caligula stated that he was going to make Incitatus a consul, or one of the officials of Rome. But he wasn't able to before he was killed, and that statement may have been a joke anyway.

In any case, Caligula treated few people, and those included consuls, better than he treated his horse. Another famous man from antiquity did the same.

STEED OF WAR

EVEN FURTHER BACK IN TIME TO **344 BCE,** AN adolescent named Alexander threw a bit of a temper tantrum when his father refused to buy a horse. King Philip II wasn't interested because the horse, called Bucephalus, wasn't tame. In fact, no one could get near him.

Alexander thought he could tame the huge beast, though. He approached Bucephalus, who had a shiny black coat and a white star on his head, and spoke softly to him. Then, according to legend, he turned the horse away from the sun so that he couldn't see his shadow. What, shadows can be scary!

Bucephalus calmed right down and the boy and the horse became lifelong companions.

As he grew up, Alexander of Macedonia transformed into Alexander the Great, conquering many cities and expanding his empire. Bucephalus was with him during many battles.

So beloved was the stallion that Alexander founded a city, Bucephala, named after his horse. When Bucephalus died, he was buried like any great warrior, in what is now Pakistan. Both his and Alexander's story have been told and retold for many centuries, ever since the original source about the battling horse.

WHAT FUNNY STORIES DO YOU HAVE ABOUT YOUR PET?

HAVE YOU EVER LEARNED ABOUT OTHER AMAZING ANIMALS?

THE MECHANICAL CAMEL

One man didn't have a horse to help him get through the desert, but he did have his own two hands and engineering skills. With these, he would build a life-saving machine, though it took a lot of effort and time.

WHILE OTHER PEOPLE ENJOY PAINTING, PLAYING soccer, or swimming laps in indoor pools, French electrician Emile Leray has a hotter hobby. He likes driving across the Sahara desert!

You might know that the Sahara, located in North Africa, is the largest hot desert in the world and stretches about as wide as the whole United States. So, driving across it isn't just something you do on a rainy Sunday afternoon. In fact, the Sahara gets very little rain at all.

"Eh, that's not going to stop me," Emile says. "Just like it didn't on my previous excursions."

In March of 1993, he packs up his vehicle— a Citroen 2CV which looks like a souped-up punch bug—and heads out from the city of Tan-Tan in Morocco.

Soon, nothing but the vast desert stretches for many miles on all sides of him. There's not only a lot of sand, but rocky out-crops and dry valleys nestled between mountains. It's beautiful but Emile also knows that it's one of the harshest climates on earth for humans to survive.

He's about 25 miles away from Tan-Tan when he comes upon a military outpost managed by the Moroccan army.

"I hope they don't try to prevent me from finishing the rest of my trip," Emile thinks aloud.

But that's exactly what the Moroccan army does. They stop Emile and ask him a few questions. They want him to turn back around and go back to Tan-Tan and more than that, they want him to take a soldier back to town with him.

"Uh, sorry guys," Emile says. "My insurance for this vehicle doesn't allow me to take passengers. Besides, it's already loaded down with all my supplies and tools."

The soldiers are not happy with this answer. But Emile doesn't change his mind.

"Then go back where you came from," say the soldiers.

Emile turns his car around and starts heading back to Tan-Tan. As soon as he's a good distance from the military outpost, he steps down on the gas and floors it.

"I hope they don't follow me," Emile says. "Because I have a plan to get around the soldiers."

His plan involves leaving the flat road and winding his way through the desert to go around the outpost. Then, he can continue on the way to his destination.

He speeds up even more, zooming down the road until he comes to a small path jutting off the side.

"This looks like a good place to veer off." Emile turns his 2CV down the rocky route and begins a bumpy ride. He's jostled around in his car as it lumbers over the rocks and holes.

Suddenly, a large rock appears in his path.

"Yikes!"

Emile is going to fast to avoid it. His 2CV hits the rock and shudders to a stop.

"Great," he says. "Just great."

He climbs out of his vehicle and inspects it. The wheel axle has snapped and the damage isn't something he can fix. The C2V is undriveable. Emile is stranded in the Sahara desert. And it's hot out.

Luckily, he has water for several days. He also brought many tools with him for the trip, including a hacksaw. That was going to come in handy.

"Well, I can't go back on foot," Emile says. "It's too far." Plus, he could run into thieves and be hurt or worse. Since this was before the era of everyone carrying a cell phone, he couldn't call for help either.

His best option, he figured, was to make a motorcycle out of the parts of his car.

But that could take a while.

"I will have to put myself in survival mode," he says, "and make my food and drink last as long as possible."

Emile rationed his supplies, then got to work. He removed the body of the Citroen and set it up as a shelter from the sandstorms. Since he didn't have any long sleeves to protect his arms from getting burnt by the sun, he made some out of socks.

The next morning, he began to disassemble the rest of the car. He thought it would take him three days to transform it into a motorcycle. It takes twelve.

Twelve days sweating in the excruciating heat. Twelve days of sawing, hammering, and screwing. Twelve days testing the ride and falling multiple

The first time he tried to test his creation, Emile almost died.

He had kept two wheels of the C2V and put the engine in the middle. The gas fumes were aimed right at his face. There were no brakes on his makeshift vehicle, so he had to stop with his feet.

Still, his Frankensteined motorcycle was impressive. For having no garage to work in, and no plans to look at, Emile had crafted quite a bike. He called it the "Desert Camel."

Almost two weeks after his car had hit a rock and come to a stop, Emile gets on his motorcycle. He balances it as best as he can. Then he rides it away from his camp.

"It works!" Emile shouts. "It really works!"

And it's a good thing it did, because Emile had been running out of water. If he'd had to stay stranded in the Sahara for much longer, he would have died by dehydration.

Thankfully, he had just enough water left for a day's worth of riding his motorcycle. What a strange bike it was cruising through the desert. When the Moroccan police saw it, what did they think it was?

Emile hitched a ride with the police back to the nearest village. Once there, he was fined and his cleverly crafted bike was impounded, or destroyed. Why? Well, it didn't match the registration documents he carried, which were for a Citroen C2V.

After he'd recovered, Emile went to retrieve what was left of his motorcycle. He put it back together and now has a souvenir from the harrowing trip when he almost didn't make it out of the sweltering, unforgiving desert.

DO YOU HAVE ANY SOUVENIRS FROM VACATIONS YOU WENT ON?

WHAT'S THE COOLEST THING YOU'VE EVER CREATED?

THE MOST POPPABLE PRODUCT
ON THE MARKET

We wonder why Emile Leray never tried to get a patent for his motorcycle...like the inventors of bubble wrap did. Only they were looking to market it as something entirely different than what it became.

MARC CHAVANNES AND ALFRED FIELDING STOOD before their enormous heat-sealing machine and inspected their new invention. It wasn't quite what they'd envisioned but it was *something*.

"Looks pretty neat," Marc said.

"It was an interesting idea, at least," Alfred stated. "But will people buy it?"

Marc ran his fingers over the product, which consisted of two plastic shower curtains that they'd sealed together. Air had gotten trapped between the sheets, creating a bubbly texture.

"Well, unique home decorating is all the rage right now in the 1950s," Marc said. "I can absolutely see people using this as wallpaper."

The problem was, no one else saw the same vision.

Even after Marc and Alfred got a patent, or license, to produce their invention, the air bubble wallpaper didn't become much of a success.

Alfred sat at his home one evening, turning a square of the stuff in his hands. "Well, I guess my dreams of fame and fortune were just dreams after all," he said wistfully.

"Ooooh, Dad, what's that?" his five-year-old son Howard asked.

"Just something I've been working on," Alfred said.

Howard climbed up on his father's lap. "Can I see?"

Almost as soon as Howard touched the plastic paper, he couldn't resist squeezing the air bubbles with his stubby little fingers. They were just so squishy.

Alfred gave his son a sad smile when suddenly they both jumped at a loud sound.

POP!

Howard giggled in delight and squeezed more bubbles.

POP, POP!

Soon, Alfred was laughing with his son and popping the air bubbles with him.

POP, POP, POP!

What a great stress reliever. Maybe there was a use for this stuff after all...

But when Alfred met Marc back in their workshop, his business partner had different ideas. Many different ideas.

"Good brainstorming," Alfred said, "but I don't see many of these working out..."

"Yeah," Marc said. "I think the most promising use of our invention might be for greenhouse insulation."

Since there are many plants that can't survive cold weather, they are often grown in greenhouses, are kept warm. Their bubble wrap could potentially be used to keep cold air out so the plants would thrive.

Alfred and Marc tested their invention in greenhouses, but it didn't insulate them very well.

By this point, both of them were pretty disappointed with their product.

"Maybe we should just give up and work on something else," Marc said.

Neither of them wanted to do that, though. Three years after they first came up with their product, they founded the company Sealed Air Corp. and continued to develop bubble wrap.

Finally, they came up with a good use for it: packaging material!

Just in time, too. For the International Business Machines Corporation (or IBM, for short), was looking for a way to ship their new computers. Big computers with lots of delicate parts.

"We have the answer to IBM's problem," said Chad Stephens, who worked with Marc and Alfred at Sealed Air. "They can ship their computers without damage by using bubble wrap."

This was the perfect solution for everyone!

Marc and Alfred finally had a good use for their invention. Not just computers, but all sorts of other industries began using bubble wrap to ship their goods around the world. Sealed Air became quite a successful company.

And millions of people have discovered just how satisfying it can be to squeeze the bubbles of air after they open a package.

POP, POP, POP!

THE LANGUAGE OF FREEDOM

Some inventors, like the men who came up
with bubble wrap, are pretty creative, right?
Some writers are, too, especially those that can
craft amazing works of art without having even
attended school.

WHAT ARE THE BEST DAYS OF THE WEEK? SATURDAY
and Sunday? Most people think so. When you spend five long
days waking up early just so you can sit in a classroom for
hours toiling over schoolwork, it's natural to look forward to
the weekend, when you can sleep in, watch more television, and
play more video games.

George Moses Horton loves the weekends as well, though he
doesn't have a television. He also doesn't go to school, either,
though he's very interested in learning to read and write.

But for George, born in the American South at the tail end
of the 1700s, learning to read is not a privilege he enjoys.

Instead, as an enslaved boy, he works in the fields of his
master, William Horton. He has nine siblings, all of whom are
enslaved as well. It's a rough life.

Music, more than anything, helps him get through the
tough times.

When George is still young, William Horton moves to a farm in Chatham County, North Carolina. Here, George begins hearing sermons and listening to schoolchildren recite the alphabet. He becomes inspired to learn to read. But how is that possible for an enslaved person like him?

George memorizes the alphabet just by listening. Then, he finds some old spelling books and teaches himself the letters and words. He begins to recognize parts of words on signs outside the farm.

As he passes by the schoolhouse, he assigns the sounds of the words he'd hear to the letters in his head and, late at night, he'd carve those letters into the dirt with his finger.

You see, George has to teach himself to read in secret, or he could be in big trouble.

Besides the schoolchildren, he also listens to people reading passages from the Christian Bible and memorizes those, too.

George grows to love language and begins composing poems. Since he can't write, he stores them in his head. When his master isn't around, George recites his poetry while working in the fields.

Some of his poems are about nature and the fields where he works.

On fertile borders, near the stream,
Now gaze with pleasure and delight;
See loaded vines with melons teem–
'Tis paradise to human sight.
With rapture view the smiling fields,
Adorn the mountain and the plain,
Each, on the eve of Autumn, yields
A large supply of golden grain.

Other times, George's poetry is about yearning for freedom.

Oh, Heaven! and is there no relief
This side the silent grave—
To soothe the pain—to quell the grief
And anguish of a slave?
Come Liberty, thou cheerful sound,
Roll through my ravished ears!
Come, let my grief in joys be drowned,
And drive away my fears.

In 1814, William Horton's son James becomes George's new master. Since he had studied language, George is well-spoken. So, James sends him to sell produce at the weekly farmer's market in Chapel Hill.

You know what else is in Chapel Hill? The University of North Carolina, UNC for short.

The trip to get there is ten miles, but George doesn't mind much because it gives him time to compose and recite more poems.

Some of the UNC students hear him and pause to listen to his verse. Each time George brings his cart to the market, his audience seems to grow.

He's never had much of an audience before, outside of the farm animals and other enslaved people. So, George is glad to share his poems and the students listen to them intently. They are enraptured by the silver tongue of enslaved man.

Every once in a while, one of the college students brings George a book. This helps his reading skill grow. Even better, some of them pay George a few coins to write love poems for them.

This is another reason that George doesn't mind the long walk to the market.

He's never earned money before that's all his own. And what better way than to sell the poems he loves to compose?

Eventually, a woman comes to visit his cart.

"Hello, George," she says. "Some of the students have told me about your poems. I'd like to buy them if you have any copies."

George shakes his head. "I'm sorry, ma'am, but I don't have any poems written down. They're all up here," he says, tapping his temple.

"Oh," says the woman. "Well, that's something I can help you with. I'm Caroline Lee Hentz, the wife of one of the professors here. And I'm also an author."

Just like the students, Caroline is impressed with George's talent in poetry. She begins writing George's poems down when he recites them, then she teaches him how to write himself.

A friendship forms between the two of them and Caroline meets with George often and teaches him grammar skills, George begins to dream of a future as a poet. In 1828, Caroline helps him publish his first poem in her hometown newspaper.

The following year, she helps him publish his first book filled with his poems, titled *The Hope of Liberty*.

With that, George Moses Horton becomes the first African American to publish a book in the US South.

He takes the money from his book and poem sales and tries to buy his freedom from his master. But James Horton refuses.

However, he does agree that George can pay for his time. This means that in exchange for money, George is allowed to write and sell his poetry and work for the university.

He publishes his second book, *The Poetical Works*, in 1845. By this time, he's had two children with his wife, Martha Snipes. Yet he still can't buy his freedom, even though he appeals to others for help. Instead, he is passed down as property to James Horton's son, Hal.

Then comes the Civil War. Two years after Abraham Lincoln passes the Emancipation Proclamation of 1863, George meets with a group of Union troops who have come to North Carolina.

"Am I to correctly assume you belonged to a plantation master?" one of them asks.

George nods. "Yes," he says, "for my whole life."

"Well, not anymore," says the soldier.

George nearly falls over in disbelief. Tears spring to his eyes. After being enslaved for 68 years, he's finally free. Free to make his own way in the world, as all men and women deserve.

Traveling with the Union troops, George makes it to Philadelphia, Pennsylvania. He publishes a third book and writes poems for the newspaper, as well as stories for Sunday school.

Yet even in a Northern state, and even after the Civil War, African Americans are still treated unfairly. Some of George's later poems reflect the discrimination he experiences. But he also writes pastorals about nature.

For 17 years, until his death, he lives in Philadelphia as a free man. North Carolina remembers their talented poet, though. Chatham County celebrates George Moses Horton Day every June 28th and has declared him their Historic Poet Laureate. He's been inducted into the North Carolina Literary Hall of Fame and UNC named one of their buildings after him.

Chapel Hill also established the George Moses Horton Society for the Study of African American Poetry and a school in the county was named after him. This school has gone through many transitions and is now Horton Middle School.

IS YOUR SCHOOL NAMED AFTER SOMEONE FAMOUS? WHAT DO YOU KNOW ABOUT THEM?

WINNING THE SPACE RACE

Here we have some other famous firsts,
just like George Moses Horton.
Only these next fellas raced each other
to become national heroes.

YOU MIGHT RACE WITH YOUR SIBLINGS TO SEE WHO can reach the front door first or maybe at school, you race to see who can get finished with their project first.

Well, starting in 1955, two countries launched a really big, really long competition: the Space Race.

It was between the Soviet Union and the United States, each of which wanted to prove their advancements in science and technology. Who would put the first satellite in space? Who would put the first person into space? Let's find out!

Rocket technology became a priority after World War II. America announced that they would put satellites into orbit and the Soviets took up the challenge soon afterward. They even pushed their commission to put a satellite into space before the US got the chance.

And they made it.

The Soviets put the first satellite, Sputnik I, into orbit in October 1957.

With this, they pulled ahead of the Americans, who launched their first satellite, the Explore I, four months later.

Now they shifted their focus to getting people into space.

While America got busy training astronauts, the Soviet Union chose 20 pilots from the air force to enter the cosmonaut training program in their country. Among these pilots was Yuri Gagarin, a very skilled senior lieutenant, which is exactly what the Soviets were looking for.

But Yuri was also quite short. He was only 5'2" which meant that he could fit inside the small capsule better than most of the others.

Yuri began preparations for going up in the Vostok 1 spacecraft, which barely had room for him after all the electronics and supplies were packed inside. He trained hard and the Soviets pushed him to beat the Americans into space.

Did they manage to come in first again?

You bet they did.

On April 12, 1961, the Vostok 1, with Yuri inside, was launched from Kazakhstan.

"Poyekhali!" Yuri yelled into the radio as he lifted off. This phrase is similar to "Let's roll!" in English.

In just a few minutes, his spacecraft entered the orbit and Yuri looked down at Earth through a window near his feet.

He was the first person to see the planet from that far away.

Remember the circumnavigators that tried to go around the world in ships, planes, or by foot?

Well, Yuri was the first person to go around the world in a spacecraft. Traveling in the Vostok 1, he made a full orbit of the globe, then prepared to come back to Earth.

That was easier said than done, though.

The spacecraft was supposed to jettison, or abandon, its equipment module when it was time to land. Which it did, but there was a problem.

The module didn't completely detach from the rest of Vostok 1. It stayed attached by some wires and added extra weight to the craft that hadn't been planned for.

Yuri began spinning around, experiencing extreme gravitational force, also called G-force. Thankfully, he was a fighter jet pilot, so he knew how to brace himself for this. He remained conscious until the wires broke and his descent back into Earth's atmosphere was stabilized.

Following his training, Yuri waited until he was a little over 4 miles above the ground. Then, he ejected from the spacecraft and opened his parachute.

A farmer and his young daughter watched the Vostok 1, looking like a round metal ball, smash into the ground. Then, they spotted Yuri, in his orange space suit, floating down from the sky.

The farmer grabbed his daughter and pulled her back in fear.

"Don't be afraid," Yuri said, after he landed. "I'm a Soviet citizen like you. I just came back from space and I must find a telephone!"

Yuri was the first person in space, but that didn't mean the Space Race was over.

The US sent their astronaut, Alan Shepherd, into space just three weeks later, though he didn't orbit Earth like Yuri had. It would take another year for John Glenn to be the first American to do that.

The Apollo Moon program was also being worked on in the US, with the hopes of putting the first man on the moon before the Soviets. At the same time, the Gemini program was developing advanced technology to upgrade American spacecrafts.

After several years of work, the Apollo 11 headed into space on July 16, 1969. Who was on board? Neil Armstrong, Buzz Aldrin, and Michael Collins.

It took them three days to reach the moon.

Once there, Neil and Buzz got into their Lunar module and descended from the Apollo 11. As Neil Armstrong stepped onto the surface of the moon, he said, "That's one small step for man, one giant leap for mankind."

The Space Race propelled people to explore outside of our planet, but it's important to know that it wasn't just one successful mission after another. There were many crashes of spacecrafts during other flights. Several astronauts and cosmonauts lost their lives as they tried to make history with space firsts.

A few years after the moon landing, the Soviet Union and the United States began to collaborate instead of compete. They set up a join project and ended the Space Race altogether.

Eventually the Soviet Union collapsed and 15 countries were separated, including Russia and Ukraine. But they still celebrate their national hero, Yuri Gagarin, the first man in space and the first to orbit the earth. Just as America celebrates Neil Armstrong, their first astronaut on the moon.

The future of space travel holds many more firsts, though it's better if we don't race to make them. Taking time to develop safety measures and solid plans will save lives and give us more information about the world beyond our own.

THE GREAT MOLASSES FLOOD

If only safety protocols and tests had been
conducted in Boston over a century ago,
when a totally preventable disaster caused
many deaths and injuries.

WHEN A GROUP OF UNDERGRADUATE STUDENTS AT Harvard University unveiled their project depicting an unusual event, Nicole Sharp was intrigued. As an aerospace engineer, she was helping teach the class. She couldn't wait to see what the students had created.

"Are all the high-speed cameras set up?" one of the students asked.

"Yep," said another.

"Great, here we go."

Nicole inspected the tiny model of the city of Boston that the students had made out of cardboard. It was quite well done and must have taken them a long time.

Yet as the cameras rolled, the students poured corn syrup onto their project.

The liquid flooded through the streets and alleys, destroying the buildings they'd carefully crafted.

What exactly were they demonstrating? Well, their project was a depiction of the Great Molasses Flood of Boston that happened in 1919.

Back then, molasses, which is a substance similar to syrup, was in demand. When fermented, it turned into industrial alcohol, which was used during World War I. After the war, it was used in the production of grain alcohol

The United States Industrial Alcohol company had set up a storage tank to hold molasses on Commercial Street in Boston, Massachusetts. It was a huge tank, about 50 feet high and 90 feet around.

This tank could hold about 2.5 million gallons of molasses!

Well, if it had been built well, it could.

Unfortunately, the tank had been crafted very quickly. It made lots of strange noises and molasses used to leak from cracks in the sides. Children even used to bring cups up to the cracks and get themselves some sweet molasses to eat.

It seems that no one knew just how dangerous this was.

During lunchtime on January 15th, the humongous molasses tank burst.

As people tried to run away, more than two million gallons of molasses swept through the city like a tsunami wave. There's a saying about being "as slow as molasses" but the liquid that spilled in Boston moved at about 35 miles per hour. One witness said it looked like burning hot oil.

The wave was up to 40 feet high in places and 160 feet wide, bringing on a "sweet, sticky death."

It took down buildings, swallowed up automobiles and horses, and knocked out the supports for elevated trains. Any rescue efforts were slowed down because the molasses was so hard to wade through.

Twenty-one people lost their lives in the flood and at least 150 were injured.

It took many weeks to clean up the mess, and people said that some parts of Boston smelled like molasses for decades after the event.

After the catastrophe, some people filed lawsuits, claiming that the tank had been shoddily built and was unsafe. Not wanting to be responsible, the United States Industrial Alcohol company said that some evil people must have sabotaged the tank.

It was a silly accusation, though it would take six years before the ruling came for the company to pay for damages their carelessness had caused.

As horrendous as the Great Molasses Flood was, it prompted people to set up better codes of construction and safety.

And for students like Nicole's at Yale University, it became a study in physics. Through experiments, they were able to understand how a liquid like molasses could cause so much destruction. You see, the cold temperatures of winter in Boston made the molasses thicker, so that rescuers weren't able to get to victims in time.

Hopefully, a disaster such as this one won't be repeated. We all need to be careful and make sure we build things sturdily so we don't risk people's lives.

ANGELS OF THE DEEP SEA

Just like molasses, water in huge quantities like an ocean can be dangerous. But one woman was more concerned about the animals swimming in the water—and their sharp teeth that she hoped wouldn't bite her.

A BOAT CARRYING FOUR PASSENGERS, INCLUDING a young woman named Yvonne Vladisavich, zooms over the waves of the Indian Ocean in 1972.

"Won't be long before we get to the island," says one of Yvonne's traveling companions.

Yvonne nods, enjoying the ocean breeze. She loves the water and ever since they left the coast of Mozambique, she'd been having a great time.

But that was all about to change.

Soon, the boaters hear a strange noise, and the small cabin cruiser shudders, then slows way down.

"What's happening?" Yvonne asks.

No one answers her as the boat comes to a complete stop.

Finally, one of the other passengers says, "I think the engine failed. I don't know what we're going to do."

"I guess we have to wait here until someone comes by to save us," says another one.

Yvonne gets worried. Everywhere she looks is the blue expanse of water. And though she loves it, she doesn't want to be stranded out in the middle of the ocean with no way to get to their destination or head back to Mozambique. She would do anything to get back to land right now.

But the universe has other plans.

The cabin cruiser begins to rock as the waves grow more intense. Yvonne sees two of her friends look in terror at something behind her.

She whips around just in time to see a huge wave come crashing down on top of them.

Yvonne is tossed into the sea and plunges underwater. She kicks frantically, hoping to get to the surface so she can breathe. Her foot comes into contact with something sharp. Yvonne winces in pain as it slices into her skin.

But she keeps kicking.

Struggling to reach the surface, she uses her arms and legs to propel herself toward the light she can see streaming in the water. Finally, her head breaks free and she gasps for air.

The cabin cruiser had overturned and is sinking fast.

Yvonne shouts for her friends, but no one answers. She feels the water around the sinking boat trying to drag her down with it and she's forced to swim away.

Luckily, she's a strong swimmer.

But does that really matter when she has nowhere to swim to safety?

Once the boat is completely out of sight, Yvonne treads water, wondering which way she should start moving. Every direction looks the exact same.

She has a stinging foot, aching legs, and a cold body. She tries to block everything else out and just focus on making forward progress.

But soon, she's tired.

So tired...

She's thirsty, too, but of course, she can't drink the salt water.

A short time later, her legs begin to feel heavy. She wishes she could curl up and rest and she wishes her injured foot would stop throbbing.

Not only did it hurt, but she was afraid that the blood seeping into the water from the wound would call any nearby sharks.

Her eyelids flutter with exhaustion, and Yvonne tells herself that she must stay awake. She must!

She floats on her back for a while to give her legs a rest, but then she feels movement in the water.

Yvonne glances around frantically.

Sure enough, there's the unmistakable triangle of a shark fin. All thoughts of being tired flee her mind. She must get out of there or she'll be dinner for some big, hungry fish.

INCREDIBLE STORIES FOR INQUISITIVE KIDS

Cautiously, she begins to kick her legs, not knowing or caring if she's heading in the right direction. She just can't stay in the middle of a circle of sharks!

There's no way she can outswim them, though, and her heart sinks. She stops swimming and awaits her fate.

Something hard and smooth presses into her stomach from below. Yvonne thinks its one of the sharks and she shuts her eyes and waits for the terrible teeth to close around her.

But this doesn't happen.

A trilling sound reaches her ears and she opens her eyes.

There's a dolphin! Actually no, there's *two* of them.

So, those fins weren't from the sharks after all? A quick glance lets her know that she hadn't been wrong before. The sharks are still there, a little farther away from her now. The two dolphins have positioned themselves between her and the predators.

It's like they're guarding her.

One of the dolphins nudges her with its sleek, rubbery nose. A chill of gratitude rushes through Yvonne. She fights back tears as she realizes the dolphins are risking their own safety to help her.

With renewed energy, she begins to swim and the dolphins take up their posts on either side of her. No sharp teeth sink into her legs, no hungry shark drags her down underwater.

Yvonne loses track of time as she swims. Her body eventually feels numb, and though she's glad her lungs and legs aren't aching anymore, she knows that she can't go on like this forever. Who knows how far away she is from land?

At some point, she stops moving and feels herself slipping underwater. But one of the dolphins pushes her back up to the surface and supports her until she can keep her head above water on her own.

She keeps going, knowing that she doesn't want to die when she's still so young. A pang of sorrow fills her as she thinks about her friends that must have sank with the boat.

It feels like she's been swimming for days. At the very least, it's been many hours. She doesn't know if she can fight the exhaustion for much longer.

Then she sees something wavering in front of her. It's shaped like an upside-down ice cream crone. It's a floating metal buoy and she tells herself that she has to reach it...

Yvonne drums up whatever strength she has left and propels herself toward the buoy. Once she gets to it, she hardly has any energy left to pull herself up on it.

Her fingers are stiff and her legs are shaking as she clings to the buoy, happy to be out of the water.

Her dolphin saviors circle around the buoy below. Every now and then, their heads poke out of the water like worms in a garden.

"I'm okay," she says to them, "thanks to you two." Her voice is hoarse, but she hopes the dolphins understand.

She feels herself dozing, but tries to remain awake. There's no way she can miss the chance to be saved. And finally, she sees a crabbing boat coming toward her.

Weakly, Yvonne raises an arm and waves.

The crabbing boat comes to her aid. As she's hauled aboard, she realizes her throat is parched. She can't wait to get a drink.

But first...

Yvonne grasps the railing of the crabbing boat, peering into the water. There they are—the two finned guardian angels who helped her survive.

"Thank you," she calls. "Thank you so much for your help!"

The engine of the crabbing boat fires up and begins to move away from the buoy. Still, Yvonne calls out her gratitude. Even over the sound of the engine, she hears the soft trill of a final goodbye.

HAVE YOU EVER BEEN IN A SITUATION IN WHICH YOU FELT HOPELESS?

HOW DID YOU GET OUT OF IT? DID ANY- ONE HELP YOU?

PLANTING FOR A PURPOSE

Just as inspiring as Yvonne Vladisavich are two men from China who are changing the environment, despite the extreme challenges both of them face.

MORE THAN TEN THOUSAND TREES. THAT'S HOW many Jia Wenqi and Jia Haixia have planted over the years together. And that's an amazing feat on its own, but even more amazing is that Wenqi has no arms and Haixia cannot see.

But it doesn't matter. For when they work together, they've managed to build a whole forest.

"I am his hands and he is my eyes," Haixia says. "We are good partners."

The two Chinese men have always been close, ever since they attended school together. They have helped each other over many decades and continue to do so, all while helping others at the same.

When Wenqi was three years old, he touched an electric cable that was on the ground. The wires were unprotected and it gave him a high voltage shock. Wenqi had to have both of his arms amputated, or removed.

Since he was so young when this happened, Wenqi doesn't really remember a time without arms.

He always just tried to do what the other children did, whether it was playing or swimming. He has adapted to life quite well, even though he has no arms. At work, he holds a plough with his neck and shoulders, and he can even write and do needlework with his feet.

Haixia, who is one year older, was born with no sight in his left eye. Then, in the year 2000, he was working in a factory when a stone fragment hit his right eye. Since then, he's been completely blind.

It was hard for Haixia to adjust to having no vision. He was very depressed. When the factory accident happened, his son was only four years old and Haixia's wife couldn't work because of illness. So, the family had no way to make money.

That's when he got back together with Wenqi. Neither of them wanted to sit around and do nothing all day, so they began to brainstorm.

"There weren't a lot of options for us. But being alive means to have a purpose. So we said to each other, 'Let's plant trees!'."

Just outside of Beijing, China, is the men's village, called Yeli. The land around Yeli had been deforested, meaning that many of the trees had been cut down. This has caused environmental damage and leads to flooding.

Wenqi and Haixia lease a plot of land from the government and go out every day to plant trees, just like they have for many years. Haixia carries a hammer and a metal rod, and hangs onto Wenqi's empty sleeve. Wenqi leads him through the forest of trees they've planted so they can plant more. Sometimes, Wenqi gives Haixia a piggyback ride while he wades across the river.

"Though we are limited physically, our spirit is limit-less," they say.

Their task is not an easy one. They have to take suitable cuttings from the trees they've planted in the past, and sometimes these are hard to reach. Wenqi bends down so that he can boost Haixia up with his back. The two of them have learned a lot about planting since they started. Sadly, their first batch of trees died.

Now, though, a whole forest of thousands of trees have grown tall. They provide homes for birds and other animals, along with fresh air. The land is becoming healthier thanks to these two brave, hardworking men.

The villagers didn't think that it was possible for the two of them to change the environment, but that's exactly what they did. It may have taken many years, but now the village helps Wenqi and Haixia out whenever they can by fixing their tools and trimming the weeds around the saplings, or baby trees.

A documentary was made about these extraordinary tree planters, and it was revealed that Haixia is on a waiting list to get a cornea transplant. That means he might be able to get his eyesight back.

Even if it happens, he claims he will continue to plant trees with his good friend Wenqi.

"So let the generations after us and everyone else see what two handicap individuals have accomplished. Even after we're gone they will see that a blind man and an armless man have left them a forest," the men say.

We can all take inspiration from Wenqi and Haixia and better the world, whether it's by planting trees or helping the environment in other ways. They have proven that even with disabilities, they can make a huge difference.

WHAT DIFFERENCES DO YOU WISH YOU COULD MAKE IN THE WORLD?

THERE'S NO BETTER TIME THAN NOW TO TAKE THE FIRST STEP!

CONCLUSION

As WE CLOSE THE PAGES OF THIS EXTRAORDINARY book, we hope you've been inspired by the remarkable stories and captivating adventures within. From the circumnavigators who braved the high seas to the aviators who soared through the skies, each tale has shown that with curiosity, courage, and creativity, anything is possible.

We've delved into the strange and mysterious, from the Great Kentucky Meat Shower to the curious case of Typhoid Mary, and explored unique and odd jobs from history. Keep asking questions, keep exploring, and never stop being inquisitive.

The world is full of wonders waiting to be discovered, and who knows? Maybe one day, you'll have your own incredible story to share with the world.

Until then, happy adventuring, and remember, the journey of discovery never truly ends!

LOVED THE JOURNEY?
HELP OTHERS DISCOVER IT TOO!

Before you go, we'd love to hear what you thought of the stories. Did you have fun? Learn something new?

Share your thoughts by leaving a quick review – it'll only take **10 seconds!**

Simply open your phone camera, point it at the **QR code** below, and get transported to the Amazon review page, instantly!

Just one or two sentences about what you enjoyed, the story that surprised you most or even a quick "Loved it!" really helps future readers find us.

As a small, family-run publishing business, your feedback makes a **BIG difference** and helps more inquisitive minds like you discover these incredible stories!

Thanks So Much For Being Part Of This Epic Learning Adventure!

CLAIM YOUR FREE GIFT!

Get instant access to the
exclusive audiobook!

This exclusive audiobook isn't available anywhere else!

Scan the QR code below with your phone

camera now and start listening right away!

Made in the USA
Las Vegas, NV
27 October 2024

10289677R00066